what I have to say I c'annot
put in words – but you know
it I am the scene –

Courage – Courage – well
we have shown that we have
it – I hope it will lead us
on our way – which is now
a little stony – –

God bless you my darling –
My thoughts are with you
and my feelings are
deep and warm – as
your Husband Richard
— xxx x

THIS WAS
RICHARD TAUBER

Richard Tauber   *Drawing: G. Rabinowicz*

THIS WAS
RICHARD TAUBER

Charles Castle

In collaboration with
Diana Napier Tauber

W. H. ALLEN
LONDON & NEW YORK
1971

© Charles Castle and Diana Napier Tauber, 1971

Printed in Great Britain
for the publishers
W. H. Allen & Co. Ltd
Essex Street
London WC2R 3JG
by W. & J. Mackay & Co. Ltd, Chatham

ISBN 0 491 00117 7

With grateful thanks to my employers, BBC Television, and to my good friends Diana Napier Tauber and Helen Arnold.

CHARLES CASTLE

FOREWORD

The subject of this book is the life, loves and letters of my late husband, Richard Tauber. Charles Castle is both a good friend and a talented writer, and I have been very happy to give him access to my archives. Assisting him in the research has proved a most nostalgic journey into the past, in the course of which there came to light many incidents and facts about Richard of which I myself had no knowledge.

Charles Castle was already familiar with much of Richard's life when he started work on the book, for he had already immersed himself for more than a year in researching, writing, directing and producing a television documentary, for BBC Television's *Omnibus* also entitle *This Was Richard Tauber*.

The main aim of this book is to present a biography of complete honesty. It was my wish that it be absolutely truthful, for I am secure in the belief that the truth can in no way lessen the stature of a great singer and musician.

DIANA NAPIER TAUBER

CONTENTS

CONTENTS

PART ONE

A Voice From the Gods
1891–1930

I
PARAGONS OF PRAISE

There was a hubbub of excitement at the Austrian Embassy in London at the awaited arrival of Frau Kammersängerin Elisabeth Schwarzkopf. Amid an air an anticipation, her appearance whipped up the same enthusiasm as it might have on a First Night, but it was a spring afternoon and the beautiful soprano, who had been recording a new album of Lieder in Berlin, had flown into London for my television documentary film, *This was Richard Tauber*. It was made under the auspices of the Tom Arnold Organisation which had presented three of Richard Tauber's stage successes in the thirties and forties, for transmission by BBC television's *Omnibus*, and world-wide television networks on May 16th, 1971, to mark what would have been Tauber's eightieth birthday on that day.

This was Richard Tauber is the film from which a great deal of the research as well as comprehensive transcriptions from interviews with international personalities has made this book possible. I used extracts from five of Richard Tauber's feature films and included film he himself has shot throughout his lifetime. These private films were retained for over twenty years in remarkably good condition, by his widow Diana Napier Tauber, and they show scenes with Franz Lehar, Marlene Dietrich and Walt Disney. My specially filmed interviews with Tauber's friends and theatre colleagues, included, apart from Elisabeth Schwarzkopf, Elisabeth Bergner, Evelyn Laye, Vanessa Lee, Peter Graves, Sir David Webster, Jane Baxter, Eric Robinson, Mischa Spoliansky, Bernard Grun, Lea Seidl, Mrs Bernard Delfont (*Carole Lynne*), and Mrs Tom (*Helen*) Arnold.

As a fitting tribute for their part, E.M.I., the company which had retained Richard Tauber under exclusive contract throughout his career under the Parlophone and Odeon Labels, have issued a special long playing record of the music from my film. This disc is also called *This was Richard Tauber* (number SRS 5065).

James Robertson Justice who was to do the films introduction and narration, and to interview Elisabeth Schwarzkopf, with whom he had appeared in BBC Television's Gala Performances, produced by Patricia Foy, had only just arrived from his eyrie in Scotland where he finds sanctuary from his heavy filming demands in the company of his pet falcons. As he speaks German, Dutch, French and Italian fluently, he was equally at ease filming the German version of the film, planned for German speaking countries, the origin of Tauber's early successes where he had become known as one of the finest tenors and Mozart singers of the century. James Robertson Justice has tremendous physical stature, which at first makes him seem forbidding, but his warmth and sense of fun, his amusing anecdotes and the twinkle in his eye soon dispel any trepidation.

"You were with the Wiener Staatsoper when it paid its first visit to London in 1947, weren't you?" Robertson-Justice asked Madame Schwarzkopf, sitting in the elegant Music Room of the Austrian Embassy overlooking Belgrave Square.

"Yes," she replied, her pale blue eyes lighting up. "We were invited to go with—shall we say?—our party pieces. There was *Fidelio, Cosi Fan Tutte, Salome* and of course *Don Giovanni*, in which Richard Tauber sang Don Ottavio to my Donna Elvira.

"We had a really fine company. We were considered to be the most famous Mozart Ensemble, and I think we still are. This was due solely to the conductor Professor Josef Krips, a truly remarkable man.

"In the company, there was Ljuba Welitch, who was a very famous *Salome*, and Hilda Konetzny, who was a wonderful *Fidelio*. Then there was Hotter, Seefried, and Jurinac—and also a certain Miss Schwarzkopf, who was one of the underlings but was there all the same!" she smiled modestly, putting her hand in a feminine gesture to her immaculate blonde hair.

"The baby of the party," laughed Robertson-Justice.

"Not exactly the baby, but they couldn't really go without me, because I was their Donna Elvira, and also their Marcellina in *Fidelio*.

"But what good fortune it turned out for me—not only because I did those performances, but because I encountered Richard Tauber's famous performance as Don Ottavio and also because I was later engaged to come back to Covent Garden by Sir David Webster, so that my relationship with my not-then husband deepened," she said referring to Walter Legge.

"But Tauber had sung at Covent Garden before, hadn't he?"

"Yes," replied Walter Legge, "I had engaged him in 1938 to do *Zauberflöte, The Bartered Bride* and *Entführung (Il Seraglio)*."

No Mozart opera had been performed at Covent Garden since 1931, and Walter Legge, who had been engaged by Sir Thomas Beecham as his Assistant Artistic Director of the Royal Opera House, Covent Garden, as the result of his work on the recording of *Die Zauberflöte* with Sir Thomas and the Berlin Philharmonic, had no difficulty in inducing Sir Thomas to conduct *Die Zauberflöte,* and *Die Entführung* in 1938, and *Don Giovanni* in 1939.

Legge had heard Richard in Salzburg in 1926 and at every possible subsequent opportunity, and had long regretted the fact that the greatest Austrian tenor had never sung opera in London. Having the reins in his hands, he at once engaged Richard to sing all three Mozart operas, and also Smetana's *Die verkaufte Braut (The Bartered Bride)*. These were Richard's only operatic appearances in Britain before his tragic last appearance when he sang Ottavio with the Vienna State Opera in 1947.

"It was at this time, in 1938," laughed Walter Legge, "that John Christie of Glyndebourne made his wicked crack that, when Beecham said he was suffering from gout, he was not suffering from gout at all, but from his leg."

"Meaning *Walter* Legge!" explained Schwarzkopf, laughing.

"And that the Mozart opera was no longer to be called *Zauber*flöte but *Tauber*flöte!"

Born in London in 1906, Walter Legge was the first record producer. At twenty he joined the staff of His Master's Voice, but was dismissed as "unsuitable" after three months. Within a year he was re-engaged to run HMV's newly formed Literary Department, which involved devising advertising material, editing the Company's trade magazine and writing "album notes".

At the age of twenty-four he founded the first record club, a subscription scheme for recording the songs of Hugo Wolf. The success of this venture was such that he developed the subscription system at an astonishing rate. Within a year, Schnabel was engaged to record the complete piano works of Beethoven.

During the war, Legge organized concerts for British troops and war workers, at first in England and then, as the war went on, in France, Belgium, Holland and Germany. As a recreation during the war years, he founded and rehearsed a String Quartet, which he developed immediately after the war into the famous Philharmonia Orchestra, soon to be built by him into one of the world's greatest orchestras; the orchestra which both Toscanini and Richard Strauss chose for their only post-war concerts in London. With the exception of Bruno Walter, Ernest Ansermet, Erich Kleiber and Koussevitsky, every great conductor in the world was associated with Walter Legge's Philharmonia Orchestra.

Between 1946 and his retirement in 1964, Legge helped to give London, through his Philharmonia Concert Society, a musical life of a richness unequalled by any other European city. It was his hobby, though. His main occupation was as Recording Manager for EMI.

In 1946, Legge toured all the accessible Western and Central European countries to negotiate and sign exclusive contracts for EMI. Within a few weeks he had completed contracts with Furtwängler, von Karajan, Kubelik, Krips, Lipatti, Edwin Fischer, Ginette Neveu, Irmgard Seefried, his wife Elisabeth Schwarzkopf and countless others.

Among Legge's exceptional recording achievements are *Tosca*, with Callas, di Stefano, Gobbi and de Sabata; *Der Rosenkavalier*, with Schwarzkopf, Ludwig and von Karajan; and *Tristan und Isolde* with Flagstad, Suthaus and Fischer-Dieskau. There is also the incomparable series of the great Viennese operettas, where he employed some of the greatest opera singers of our time to lend their experience and lustre in a demonstration of the true values as well as the magic of Johann Strauss' stage works.

Legge resigned from EMI in 1964, after nearly forty years of devotion to the building of a unique and priceless catalogue. He told me that changes in the administration had made it impossible for him to carry out his artistic plans; and that because he found it impossible to maintain the standards he had achieved with his Philharmonia Orchestra and Chorus, he decided to leave England and settle in Switzerland. The only recordings he has produced in the last six years are those made by his wife, Elisabeth Schwarzkopf.

"Richard never rehearsed with us," Schwarzkopf continued, looking remarkably poised and fresh for one who had just arrived in London from Berlin after a tiring week in recording studios. "He had neither piano nor orchestra rehearsals, for *Don Giovanni* was the final performance of the season and there simply wasn't time."

"Richard had probably not sung opera for seven or eight years because he hadn't been back to Vienna after 1938, and I don't think he sang opera anywhere at that time," said Legge.

"So he sang it cold, so to speak?" observed Robertson-Justice.

"Yes, cold" Schwarzkopf replied, "after quite a few years of singing operetta, conducting, composing, touring America, Australia, South Africa and of course Europe. Besides, he was an extremely ill man. Though none of us knew that at the time; he gave no indication of it whatsoever.

"Even so, I had never heard any tenor sing with this beauty of tone before, plus the control, the breathing control, the expression, and the clean intonation. I could go on and on about the plusses. I don't think that any of us in the company had ever come across— much less been on the stage with—a singer of the calibre of Richard Tauber. It was something we had never encompassed in Vienna. We were cut off from this kind of singing and so when we heard that we were to sing one performance with him—well, imagine our excitement."

"It has been said in criticism that his singing had too much—schmaltz," provoked Robertson-Justice.

"Schmaltz? No. It hadn't," Schwarzkopf replied firmly. "I think people were entirely mistaken. He had an individual, most sensual sound—not an arid voice, but a fantastic sound. He was really the greatest tenor I had the fortune to hear—or for that matter to sing with—and there is no better way of describing his way of making music with his voice than by comparing him to the great violinist Fritz Kreisler.

"I was lucky enough to meet Kreisler once in New York, but I had never heard him except on records. The first time I heard him was when my husband played one of his records. I was on the top floor of our apartment, and he played it downstairs. I raced down three floors. I had never heard such an individual sound on the violin before. Oistrach, for instance, has said that Kreisler was the king of violinists because of that wonderful individual sound, coupled with rubato, rhythm, expression and so on. The same applied to Richard. It was this God-given individual sound, plus a fantastic musical capacity and mind to work. He had to overcome great difficulties, physical handicaps—which we all have, in a way. But when I sang with him, I don't remember being aware of any of those physical handicaps. I just listened to that voice. After all, I stood in front of him throughout the aria and I was close enough to study his breathing. It was a fantastic lesson, listening to this remarkable sound which I had only ever heard from Fritz Kreisler."

Richard brought character to his Mozart roles, whilst singing with purity of tone and perfection of phrase. In his opening recitative and aria 'On her Contentment', from *Don Giovanni*, he gave polished and significant expression to Ottavio's moods.

"Those of us who have heard the famous tenor only through his records and films," a music critic wrote, "expected to find a voice of greater power and range, but though his range of expression on the stage was on a smaller scale, it was no less convincing. He did not lose in his contraction the subtlety of transition which was the great wealth of his singing. The thrilling use of soft tones was never more frequently exemplified in singing than by him. Sometimes a line would open unexpectedly, with a soft tone of such mellowness as to give a sense of loveliness and ravishment at the onset. At other times the emotion of cadences would be enhanced by some lovely final or penultimate note, in which the art of refined tone and exquisitely controlled breath were so perfectly blended that the tone had softness of the purest beauty."

Another music critic reported his *Don Giovanni*: "He sings the two arias incomparably; how he gives by the power of his cantilena the end of the G Major aria a soaring poised line to that baroque, octave-leaping melody; how he fills the colorature of the B Major flat aria with his dramatic life is quite unprecedented. It has never happened before that Don Ottavio, a figure which usually remains in the background, was received with such a storm of applause and that Don Giovanni himself should have been overshadowed."

That Vienna State Opera Season was arranged by Sir David Webster, now retired as General Administrator of the Royal Opera House, Covent Garden.

On his retirement in 1970, singers including Joan Sutherland, Tito Gobbi, Geraint Evans, Amy Shuard and Peter Glossop, and the conductors George Solti, Colin Davis, Edward Downes and John Pritchard paid their tribute to him in extracts from his favourite operas in a Gala Performance at the Royal Opera House on June 30th 1970, in the presence of Her Majesty Queen Elizabeth, the Queen Mother, and His Royal Highness the Prince of Wales. Lord Drogheda, Chairman of the Royal Opera House paid tribute to Sir David at the end of the performance.

As far as I was concerned Sir David had paid his own tribute to Richard three months before, from the Royal Box, where I filmed him, while below in the orchestra pit George Solti was conducting the rehearsal of *Falstaff*, a production which was to have such a tremendous reception on the Royal Opera's first German tour in 1970 with Geraint Evans and Regina Resnik as leading singers:

"Tauber was a typical Viennese with all the Viennese charm," Sir David said, "with all the Viennese lightness and capacity for transferring, for putting across humour, and of course, he had the most magnificent and beautiful lyric voice. I have no hesitation in saying that he was one of the greatest lyric tenors of the age. He had the most enormous charm, which he could put across in the theatre, and this was quite a considerable achievement, because he was lame, and you'd have thought that a figure on the stage being lame would have detracted from his performances; but it didn't. The charm and the ability to be liked came over in all his performances."

But what made him one of the greatest tenors—one of the finest Mozart singers—of his time? What drove him through his extraordinary career from the opera stages in Vienna and Berlin to musical comedy in London? From an early beginning as a music student, to an early end at fifty-eight as an accomplished singer, concert conductor and composer of love songs?

Throughout his career, he was willing to sing anything that was within his range and not likely to damage his voice. He had made his reputation on his middle voice, which was so right for German singing. But there was no public in England for his opera singing during the war years; his audiences wanted his light operetta and musical comedy, to lighten the wartime bombing and misery.

He was a polished musician, who not only knew the part he was singing but everyone else's, so that his performance was created from the complete work. This is extremely important with Mozart. He had made an exceptional character study of Don Ottavio and gave the nobleman, rather unkindly handled in the opera, a certain gutsy toughness.

But his first Mozart rôle was that of Tamino in *The Magic Flute* thirty-five years before in Chemnitz in Germany; the performance that led him to a brilliant opera career and contracts with the Vienna State Opera, the Royal Opera House Covent Garden, the Albert Hall and Carnegie Hall.

The London Philharmonic Orchestra

Richard was in his element touring as conductor with the London Philharmonic Orchestra, in the forties, and taking over the Thomas Beecham Sunday concerts at the Albert Hall.

Felix Aprahamian, Music Critic of the *Sunday Times*, believes that Richard was one of the finest conductors with whom the London Philharmonic Orchestra had ever worked.

"I think that after nearly thirty years this is forgotten," Aprahamian said, "but the players who played under him certainly remember".

"Tauber knew his scores by heart, and never referred to them
whilst conducting, but that's quite common these days. The point
about his memorizing was that he really knew every note of every
score that he conducted, and this instantly commanded the musicians' respect. I don't think it is realized today that though this man
who was so successful as a singer in Mozart and in musical comedy,
his performance of, say, Beethoven's Pastoral Symphony was
rated by the players on the same plane as the performances of that
work by Beecham or Erich Kleiber. This was the class of musician
and category in which Tauber belonged.

"He did his best work with the London Philharmonic Orchestra
during the war years, when Beecham was away and the orchestra
played in London, but also more frequently in provincial tours,
and that's where audiences and orchestra responded to the warmth
of his interpretation. He was a very, very remarkable orchestral
conductor."

His style of direction was trenchant and masterful. He inspired
orchestras to displays of disciplined vitality which evoked ovation
upon ovation from crowded auditoriums. Translated in terms of
instrumental technique, his buoyant rhythms and imaginative
command of phrasing produced attractive effects of improvisation.
He insisted upon virile and unanimous responses from all sections
of the orchestras and exacted such picturesque gaiety of tone in
merry passages and such orderly refinement of string and wood-
wind playing in slow movements as conveyed the full spirit of the
music.

Good Luck—Bad Fortune

Richard married twice, and had a roving eye. "A piano and a
beautiful girl is all I need—then I am happy!" he said. He had a
unique restlessness for world travel, with no desire for a home of
his own. He had spent his life in hotels and apartments, travelling
on boats, performing on stages. A man with no capacity for saving,

he was extravagant, and generous to a fault. He died in debt to the Inland Revenue to the tune of £22,000.

Hitler brought an end to his singing career in Berlin, where he was accepted as the Caruso of Germany; and cancer of the lung brought an end to a life of unending struggle, from the moment when he was born out of wedlock to a Roman Catholic mother and a Jewish father.

Richard's London ear, nose and throat specialist, who has treated many great opera singers and famous pop singers, was present when the surgeon, Lord Brock, diagnosed Richard's fatal illness. His name is withheld for professional reasons.

"When I was a young student," the doctor told me in his Harley Street surgery, "I admired Richard Tauber's Mozart singing enormously and I was thrilled when the opportunity to meet him arose. It was almost forty years ago now, but I remember the circumstances very well.

"He was at the height of his fame, and I was a young House Surgeon, training at a large hospital in Vienna. Richard's first wife, Carlotta Vanconti, who had pretended to commit suicide, had been admitted to our hospital. It wasn't a very serious attempt and she was now recovering.

"Rather late one night, possibly after a performance, Richard suddenly appeared at the hospital. I was on duty, and escorted him to the ward. Afterwards he came to see me in my duty room. Under the strain of the circumstances of his visit, he was obviously pleased to have found an admirer of his, and we soon started talking about music and his Don Ottavio in particular. He looked at me and asked whether I was happy in my work. I told him I was, and he replied: 'The trouble with choosing music as a career is that in order to lead the sort of life which you would enjoy, you've got to be very lucky; very fortunate indeed.'"

And throughout his career, he was.

"The one quality which struck me most in the years I came to know him, was his modesty," the doctor continued, "He never threw his weight about, he was always gentle, and he had a childlike simplicity. He was fond of using words which didn't exist—that he had made up himself. Words like *schnulpe* and *schnappula*—which were words he used to describe practically anything!"

Physically he was somewhat handicapped. He had suffered from an attack of arthritis in the late twenties which had left him with stiffness in the right knee and wrist joints. "To me, it was always extraordinary to what lengths he would go to conceal these disabilities, which really could never have affected his singing or his artistry.

"When he made his entrance on the stage for instance, he would walk with a little jumping step in order to conceal the limp, and when he was conducting, he was anxious that the audience, and the orchestra, should not notice that his wrists did not move as freely as they should."

In fact Richard was so afflicted that he was incapable of shaving himself, and relied on the services of barbers wherever he went.

Diana Napier Tauber, Richard's strikingly attractive widow, lives in a charming house that was once an orangery overlooking a walled rose garden in Berkshire. She bought the house with the proceeds of a film in which Richard's music was used, and had appropriately chosen the grounds for the new Richard Tauber Garden Theatre; but with the support of her local Bracknell Development Corporation, a site incorporating an Arts Centre has been selected instead. Sitting in her garden, she spoke to me frankly and without restraint:

Letters of Redress

"Richard had a very complicated character," she said. "He had been brought up by his father to believe that by going to bed with a woman he could contract syphilis, which would affect his brain and voice, rendering him incapable of singing. It was a tragic old wives' tale that had been drummed into him since early youth. I turned to Siegmund Freud in Vienna for help, but he told me that it was impossible to help Richard, for his complex was too deeply-rooted.

"When war separated us in 1940, Richard, left alone, soon

found girl friends, and was unfaithful. I admit I fell in love with other men too, but we never lied to each other. We accepted the fact as a hazard of war.

"Richard's loyalty was amazing. He supported and cared for the women he loved to the end of his life, with the exception of his first wife Carlotta Vanconti whom he felt he had every reason to reject. Yet, for all his love affairs, he mistrusted women. He felt they loved him for his money, his fame, or, as he would say with a wry smile: 'For my Top C.'

"He had practically everything against him: a limp, a squint from birth, his wrists were stiff with rheumatism, he was very fat, and when I first met him he ate like a small boy, gobbling his food and tucking the napkin under his chin!

"We never stopped loving each other even though in his loneliness he chose the arms of another woman after I left to join the Polish army.

"I remember a particular event that almost ended our marriage. It was in 1942, and I had been posted to Scotland two years before. Richard had fallen in love with Esther Moncrieff, an extremely beautiful girl with dark hair and a sweet natural smile, ten years younger than I."

Esther had a part in *Old Chelsea*, in which Richard had toured prior to its London Première. The show was due to open in Edinburgh—Diana's base. The following two letters between Diana and Richard reveal the situation:

Linlithgow, Scotland.
1942

My dearest Richard,

I know you have been unhappy, alone and miserable these last two years. I know I left you in London in 1940, and you suffered alone until the end of that year when you met Esther. You can't bear to be alone, Richard, I realize that, but there is a war on and I had to do something. I had to join up since we were given British Nationality. Well, I accepted Victor Cazalet's offer to help the Poles because I spoke a little German and French. You agreed that it was a good idea, and you were pleased for me to be in uniform.

As you know, dearest, we came to terms with the absence in 1940 when you told me you had met this sweet beautiful girl, and you were honest. Very honest. But what could I do stationed in Scotland in charge of a Unit of 120 girls; I couldn't just run out and say "Richard is being unfaithful; I must leave my Unit; I must get demobbed." Of course I could not, so I agreed to understand.

I agree, I had left you alone in very bad times, and it was either my fault, or the fault of this horrid war. Anyway, it was something we could not help. But Richard, there are limits. You cannot bring this girl and live openly with her in the area where I am stationed and where I work. It's not fair, and we are not in Austria. We are in England, and English people look differently on morals. I simply can't let you do this to me; it's too insulting, and the terrible thing is that you don't see it. Oh yes, Richard, I love you and I always will. I can't help it, but I think we must divorce, otherwise how can we go on? I am young; I want a life too, a home and family before it's too late. Your girl friend seems a nice girl and I am sure you are happy with her, so why not divorce? Surely we could be friends and I would then be free to make a new life for myself.

Please Richard dearest, I do love you. I want to remain your wife but you can't visit me where I am well known and respected; you can't do it—you just can't.

My love and deep feelings, Richard. Please think before you force me to an action I am sure I will be sorry for, as somehow I have always felt you needed me and I need you. There is something so strong between us, yet I don't know, I am so very unhappy, and I try so hard to find other amusements, other men, but deep inside me, there is only you.

Your loving wife,
Diana.

To which he replied:

Midland Hotel, Manchester
24th October 1942

Dearest Diana,

You cannot expect that I should let this person, who has been with me for the last two years, suffer the many difficulties which this horrible war has inflicted; I cannot send her away like a servant.

You must understand that that is impossible, no matter how you feel about her. Apart from that, it is also impossible for me to do that because you are so dear to me and I value you very much.

You know that we have come to the conviction that we should keep our marriage intact, and not be like thousands of others who have ended up with wrecked marriages through circumstances of war. I know that our ties are stronger than that, and somehow we will find a right way out. You have for two years mastered the situation with discretion and understanding. Please, please don't give up everything. You are, and you will always be my wife, dearest heart. Of course one has to have a strong will, and as long as we have that, all is not lost. But if after all this you regard a divorce as the only solution, I will have to carry the burden of that, and I will carry it without complaint.

You know very well, and you have admitted, that at the moment a change in the situation would not be very good, mainly for reasons of my health. Now, more than ever for my work and our life, dearest, I hope that you will understand this letter which is written from my soul, and I hope your feelings for me will be stronger than your intelligence. My feelings for you are always the same, no matter what you decide.

> Your loving husband,
> Richard.

The show opened in London as scheduled, but providence provided Diana with a course of Army Training in Scotland and the situation was averted. But not resolved.

Richard and Esther were to become inseparable during wartime and Diana sought a posting abroad in the Army in order to save face.

II
BIRTH OF A VOICE

Richard was born on May 16th 1891 in Linz, capital of Upper Austria, a hundred and twenty miles from Vienna. His mother, Elisabeth Seiffert, a Roman Catholic, was a widow of over forty when he was born. A soubrette at the local municipal theatre, her maiden name was Denemy, and Richard was known as Carl Richard Denemy until the age of twenty-one, when he was formally adopted by his father, Richard Anton Tauber, the tenth child of a Hungarian Jewish merchant.

"My grandfather, Anton Tauber, was a rich wine merchant in Bratislava, the capital of Slovakia, in the middle of the nineteenth century," Richard had told Diana. "He was rich and respected; and since there were no orphanages nor welfare institutions he was relied upon for his generous donations to charity.

"With 1871 came the ill-famed Black Friday in Vienna when the most solid fortunes melted, and my grandfather was forced to leave Bratislava to start a new life in Vienna to support his fourteen children.

"It was during this time that my father, Richard Anton Tauber, decided to turn from the family's merchant trade to the more respected spheres of academic training. He studied Latin and Greek but each day he attended not only college, but the theatre as well and he began neglecting his studies. He would visit the Wiener Burgtheater, where from the fourth gallery he would enjoy performances of Schiller and Shakespeare with his books tucked neatly under his feet.

"He came to devote more and more time to the theatre and his studies naturally palled. He was summoned before his Head, and learned that he hadn't the slightest chance of graduating. When his father made it clear that he wasn't likely to become a lawyer nor a doctor, my father replied that he might possibly make a finer actor—a remark that was met with a clout on the ear!'"

There was a famous pawnshop called the Dorotheum in Vienna, not far from the Tauber home, so named because it was built on the site which had once been the Monastery of the Holy Order of Dorothea.

One bitterly cold winter's morning the thirteen Tauber child-ren came down to find their coats missing, and neatly pinned to the clothes hooks were thirteen pawn-tickets that the aspiring actor in the family had received from the Dorotheum in exchange for the coats. A note to father Tauber explained that son Richard Anton had secured an acting engagement at St Pölten, and deeply re-gretted having had to pledge the family's winter warmth in ex-change for the fare for his first public appearance.

By the time Richard was born, his father, who was thirty and at the height of his artistic career, was touring America as guest artiste.

"My own arrival can be explained by the fact that in 1890 Richard Anton Tauber had been engaged to appear in Graz." Richard continued. "On his return home to Prague he stayed over-night in Linz, where he met a soubrette, Elisabeth Seiffert, who was appearing at the local theatre. They dined after the show, he saw her home, and nine months later, unbeknown to the visiting actor, I was born.

"Since my mother was appearing nightly at the theatre, it was essential for her to find someone to look after me, and I was sent to a foster home when I was three days old.

"There was a town called Urfahr on the opposite side of the Danube from Linz, on the bank of the river. Semi-rural, semi-urban houses had been built at Urfahr at the end of the 18th century, and now elderly residents there earned their living by taking in foster children. My mother paid very little for my keep, but she was able to visit me daily from Linz during the day, before her evening performances.

"My foster-parents kept chickens and a pig, and it was on this modest holding, far removed from the splendour of the bourgeois rich life my father enjoyed in Prague, that I spent the first six years of my childhood.

"When I was six my mother had to leave the theatre in Linz to take up a contract at another provincial theatre, and she wrote to my father in Prague, informing him of my existence. She told him that she didn't wish to make any legal claim for my welfare, but that I needed to be looked after in her absence.

"So excited was my father at the news of a son that he took the next fast train to Linz to find me. He crossed the Danube and found me covered in mud, seized me, and transferred me to his hotel, where he had me scrubbed and newly provided with clothes.

"He decided there and then to take charge of my well-being, and this was to be the start of a new world for me."

Father and son moved to Berlin, from where the father's acting career secured him further contracts at Wiesbaden.

"By the time Richard was nine," his Father once related in an interview, "his musical talents began to show, albeit in his imagination. He'd assumed a large orchestra of his own, with drums, trumpets and brass; and *he* was the conductor. Could this have been the subconscious choice of a career which would one day achieve world fame for him?

"He won his first laurels after reciting one evening at a concert in Innichen in the Tyrol; but he was too young for me to think of initiating him into the family trade—the theatre. Besides which, a thorough education was essential.

"I sent him to high school in Wiesbaden, where I was a reasonably successful actor, and he took up the piano and violin. But he was to give up the violin when his interest in education declined—much in the way that mine had.

"I gave him the choice of careers when he was sixteen, and it was natural enough for him to yearn for the theatre. But he wanted to be a singer. Since he showed no signs of a talent for singing, I doubted that he knew his own mind."

Richard's ambition to become a singer was intensified through a friend of his father at the Wiesbaden Theatre, Heinrich Hensel, the youthful heroic-tenor. He idolized Hensel—he imitated the way

Hensel dressed, followed him wherever he went, and carried his music—naturally displaying the title-page for all to see and presume that it was he, Richard, who was the singer.

However, Richard's father had decided on a conducting career for him by now, and sent him to the music conservatoire at Frankfurt where he worked with the young Arthur Rother, second conductor of the Wiesbaden Theatre.

Richard was among the first of the pupils to conduct the Egmont Overture, but although he showed talent as a conductor he was still determined to become a singer."

"My dream came true when, as a young man, I was called upon to sing at the Frankfurt Opera House, and the distinguished Wiesbaden Court Theatre," said Heinrich Hensel, who had met Richard in 1906. "Father Tauber had become one of my closest friends, and I remember young Richard projecting glass slides through a magic lantern on to an old sheet hung on the wall. He had reflected a red beam of light onto his improvised screen, having arranged this primitive lighting in such a way as to give the room quite an extraordinarily imaginative atmosphere."

And this early interest in cinematography was to develop later when Richard bought his first 16 mm camera, which he was to carry with him throughout his world travels, filming stage productions from the wings, and friends, landscapes and scenery wherever he went.

"He became attached to me, and admired my singing," Hensel continued, "and would accompany me to the theatre, hearing my roles over and over again. He would be quite upset if I failed to get seats for him.

"Richard had his first love affair when I was singing *Armide* by Gluck. He had become infatuated with one of the beautiful young dancers who lay at my feet in the second act. But the young lady was the girl-friend of the theatre's director, and Richard's father, who valued his own position in the theatre, feared the director discovering the affair and had no alternative but to end the alliance by sending his amorous young son away to Freiburg, where he stayed with friends."

Richard continued his studies at the high school at Freiburg, and

at the Basle Conservatoire. Meanwhile his father married a widow
with two sons, Robert and Otto Hasé-Tauber, in 1910.

Lily Sarrazin, the daughter of those friends of his father with
whom Richard stayed at Freiburg, was an accomplished pianist
and encouraged Richard to continue with his singing. She arranged
an audition with Professor Carl Beines, a well-known singing
teacher in Freiburg.

"Richard Anton Tauber came to see me in 1911," recalled Professor Beines, "and introduced his son, saying that he pretended to
have a voice and insisted on becoming a singer. Would I test his
voice in the hope of discouraging him from his false illusion? So I
tested him. He sang the love-song from *The Walkure* by Wagner,
and I found his voice quiet; the height and depth were decidedly
limited, but there was a timbre in his tenor which appealed to me.
I particularly liked his musicality and temperament. So I told his
father that I felt it needed time to prove his ability, to teach him
breathing and relaxation, to teach him not to push the sounds dead,
and that he should never sing Wagner again, for it was not suited
to his voice; and only then would I be able to decide whether he
would become a singer or not."

Beines came to believe that Richard had the makings of a
beautiful *bel canto* voice, but he stipulated stern conditions and discipline if he was to make anything out of it. Strict daily exercises
were called for, as well as Richard's promise not to sing in public
for at least eighteen months.

"The more he concentrated on his daily exercises," Beines con-
inued, "the lighter and more free his voice became".

"One day he sang Beethoven's *Adelaide* so beautifully that I
told him if he continued that way, if he concentrated on his techni-
cal exercises, he would become a German Caruso; possibly one of
the greatest tenors of his time."

By now father Tauber had become manager of the Neuesstadt-
theatre in Chemnitz, and wrote to Beines on Richard's return
home. "What you have done with my son's voice is a wonder! As
an old man of the stage, I would never have believed that a voice
could unfold and develop so beautifully."

So impressed was he, in fact, that he engaged Richard to sing

Tamino in *The Magic Flute* at his theatre, in March 1913, and a few days later, Max in Weber's *Der Freischütz*. He was, however, prudent enough to arrange for Count Seebach, the director of the Dresden State Opera, to hear the performances, and this led to a five-year contract for Richard at the Dresden State Opera—after only two years of study.

Privy Councillor Hofrat Schuch, who was present at the Chemnitz performances, remarked snidely to young Richard at his Dresden first night: "You were careful in your choice of a father!"

Notes of Appeal

Richard was to show his gratitude to Beines through the years, and in time, in a reversal of roles, his help would be sought by Carl Beine's daughter, Jolantha, when she lost her left leg in an ice-skating accident.

Heidelberg
January 27th, 1932

Dear Mr Tauber,

You will be surprised to receive a letter from me. I really do not know what to do any more except to put myself entirely in your hands. I know that you are overburdened with work, but I hope you will have a few moments to spare me.

As you know, I am the youngest of the three daughters, and that I had an accident injuring my leg. This is one of the reasons my parents have encouraged me to study, so that in the future I might have a vocation and be able to keep myself.

I have taken up dentistry, and have my first exam in the summer. After this exam, I shall have three more terms to study, but unfortunately times have changed and things have become rather bad. After all deductions, my father receives only 420 marks a month and private pupils are now nonexistent. I know how economically my parents live but even so my father is not capable of paying for my studies any more. You can imagine what it would mean to me to have to give up my studies in the Spring, and I really cannot express my feelings, and my studies have helped me so much to compensate for my accident.

I have never mentioned my worries to my parents, as they have enough of their own. You know that my father has played a large part in your success in what you are today. I want to ask you if you would please consider everything and the great need I have, to help me with my studies. I will study very hard to make a success, which goes without saying, and rest assured, that I shall be grateful to you all my life.

My college costs 350 marks a term, and to live I need, even if I am terribly careful, 150 marks a month.

My parents do not know about this letter, so please send your answer to the above address before you contact my father. My poor dear old father; I feel so sorry for him as he has so many worries and anxieties, and it is so necessary that he should look after himself. He has worked and laboured all his life and the result is his old age. I hope you understand this letter in the spirit I write it.

Your grateful,
Jolantha Beines.

Richard agreed to pay for Jolantha's education, and received thanks from her father:

Darmstadt,
32 Heidelbergesser 10,
13th February 1932

My dear Richard,

You really are a very dear chap, and we have been deeply moved by a letter we received from Jolantha. She informed us to our amazement that she wrote to you saying it was impossible for me to continue paying for her studies, and she is delighted that you will pay her 500 marks for the last four terms. You are a sweet man, and we thank you very much and sincerely for this help, which takes a great worry off our shoulders.

Your faithful old friend,
Carl Beines.

Richard sent the money and received the following acknow-ledgement from Jolantha:

Heidelberg,
26th May 1932.

Dear Mr Tauber,

Yesterday I called at the bank and the money had arrived. I would like to thank you again, and I am so happy that I can con-tinue my studies.

What a pity you were unable to visit us in Darmstadt, we were all looking forward to it. Maybe the next time. Perhaps you could come via Heidelberg, as I hear you are going to England in May. I wish you great success, and remain your grateful,

Jolantha Beines.

Dark-haired, and with a cheerful disposition in spite of the obstacles she encounters with her artificial leg, Jolantha has a quick sense of humour and a philosophical approach to life. I met her recently at her home in Darmstadt, near Frankfurt, West Germany, where in Rossdorf she has a successful dentistry practice—the career she mentioned in her letter forty years before. She told me about her two marriages, and how proud she is of her twenty-eight-year-old son who is at University.

From Tadpole to Tenor

"During his study period with Carl Beines," Hensel remembered, "Richard sang to me in the Pension Mevi where he lived. I was speechless when I heard his *Bildnis* Aria; his *Don José* aria; his *Don Ottavio* aria—the free-sounding start without pressure or bad habits. Really unbelievable. I knew then that Richard would become a great singer.

"His father's dearest wish was that we should sing together, and the opportunity arose at Chemnitz, when Richard sang Lorenzo to

Richard between the ages of twelve months and eight years.

Richard as a music student at seventeen and (*right*) at eleven.

With his mother.

With his father.

(*Right*) Don Ottavio in Mozart's *Don Giovanni*.
Photograph: *Erich Lindacher*.

(*Left*) Tamino in Mozart's *The Magic Flute*.

In Donizetti's *The Daughter of the Regiment*.

Barinkay in Johann Strauss's *The Gypsy Baron*.

(*Above right*) Pinkerton in Puccini's *Madame Butterfly*.

(*Right*) Wilhelm Meister in Ambroise Thomas' *Mignon*.

Richard in 1918.   *Photograph: Bruno Wiehr.*

In Offenbach's *Tales of Hoffman* (1918).   In Wilhelm Kienzl's *The Evangelist* (1922).

Photograph: Photo-Schmidt.

With leading ladies at the Vienna State Opera (1920–26).

Lensky in Tchaikovsky's *Eugene Onegin*.

Calaf in Puccini's *Turandor*.
German Première, Dresden 1926.

my Fra Diavolo. I can still see his father sitting up there in his box, beaming!

"Richard developed as a singer with his own individual technique, and with his background and knowledge of music as a trained conductor, he didn't allow anyone to throw him. He was constructive and a master in the finale. What was more important to me was that he knew the meaning of true friendship and loyalty."

Richard's first performance in Dresden was in August 1913, as the Prince in Auber's *Masaniello* (*Die Stumme von Portici*), a role he had taken over after only three days of rehearsal. He was to develop an exceptional musical memory and the ability to learn his roles quickly, thereby enabling himself to take over coveted roles at short notice.

The years in Dresden proved to be his happiest and most carefree, through his friendship with Elisabeth Rethberg, Tino Pattiera and Lotte Lehmann, who was at that time a young beginner herself:

From her home in Austria, Lotte Lehmann contributed the following tribute to Richard to mark his eightieth birthday:

FONDACHHOF
Salzburg

14th July 1970

Richard Tauber—the sensitive, deeply musical, always changing yet remaining the same marvellous wonderful artiste—
Richard Tauber—the dear and good friend—
Richard Tauber—the charming and humorous, fantastic, extravagant man—that is what he was. And unforgettable.

Lotte Lehmann

"I had bought my first car in 1913," Richard said, "and Elisabeth Rethburg, Tino Pattiera and the conductor Kutschbach and I would drive for miles through villages and hamlets, singing at the top of our lungs.

"Elisabeth became my closest companion throughout my apprenticeship at the Dresden Opera, and we were often to sing together on German concert tours. Years later, on my first visit to New York in 1931, she was appearing at the Metropolitan Opera House, where I was happy to discover that international success hadn't spoiled her. She owned a beautiful house in New York where I spent many pleasant days with her, exchanging recollections of our youthful Dresden days.

"One of my dearest—that is to say, financially dearest—Dresden roles that I recall, was the small part of the First Gralsritter in *Parsifal*. The first performance at the Opera House was one of the last to be conducted by Ernst von Schuch, who died the following year in 1914.

"I had gone on a short trip to Chemnitz, where I spent Christmas Eve with my father and stepmother.

"I was to appear in a performance of *Parsifal* at five o clock on Christmas day, and the through train was due to leave Chemnitz at three, arriving at Dresden at four. My appearance wasn't until the middle of the first act, and I knew I would make it in good time. However when I arrived at the Chemnitz station it had begun snowing heavily and the Dresden train was three hours late. Naturally I panicked, and hired a taxi for the hour-long drive to Dresden. But due to the snow-storm we arrived late, and I missed my performance. The following day I was sent for by the director Baron Seebach.

"I explained my predicament and he asked how much the taxi had cost me. 'A hundred marks, Excellency', I replied—about twenty pounds these days. 'A hundred marks!' he exclaimed— Well, I think that is punishment enough. Off you go!'

"Naturally I was delighted! Another time, when Count Seebach told me that I was to sing Pinkerton in *Madame Butterfly*, I was equally pleased. But on the day I learned that Minnie Nast, who was to sing the leading rôle, refused to sing with a 'mere beginner'.

"However, the performance took place, and after our duet the audience rose in tumultuous applause.

"Minnie Nast never refused to sing with me again!"

The following year Richard came to the rescue at a performance of Carmen about which the music critic George Kaiser wrote: "Yesterday Herr Tauber sang Don José for the first time. It was the best performance he has given so far. There can be no further doubt that he will achieve the means for greater lyric tasks, if he will wait for the time until his beautiful voice gets more consistency at the top around G and A, and by really energetic practice gets over his unfortunate lisp. What he gave yesterday in tranquil *bel canto* and *parlando* was for the most part vocally and musically excellent. The second act *Flower Song* with the voice in piano leading up to the top B lyrical peak suited him wonderfully well."

This was to be followed up by a letter from Count Seebach to Richard's father:

Dresden,
26th January 1915

My dear Director,

As both of us, you as Father and I as Manager, take an equally great interest in the opera singer Tauber, I am compelled to have to inform you that the efforts which your son has for some time devoted towards remedying his faults seem to have ceased altogether. While at first I was pleased about his progress, I must now state that his notorious 'S's' are again as bad as they had been in the beginning. Moreover, he has acquired a very noticeable tremolo, which stood out at his last performance of *Carmen*. He himself has admitted that for the last fortnight he has neither attended any lessons nor done any work at home. It seems to me that he has again taken to loafing about town. I shall ask your son to come and see me and I shall try my best to influence him to mend his ways, but I think it advisable if you too were to take him to task, and that is my reason for writing to you. After all, it would be a thousand pities if thoughtlessness were to lead to a complete wastage of your son's undoubted talents.

With my compliments,
Your obedient servant,
Count Seebach.

To which Richard's father replied:

Chemnitz.
31st January, 1915

Your Excellency,

I am deeply grateful for your concern for my son's development.

After a long discussion, he has faithfully promised me that he will
prove to your Excellency in the next performance that he has by
no means relaxed his efforts to remedy his fault and he will forth-
with stop his habit of loafing about. For his performance in *Carmen*
he gives the excuse that he had taken the part over at the last
moment and therefore had been unable to plan how best to husband his vocal resources.

With compliments,
Your obedient servant,
R. Tauber.

Later that year, Richard Strauss was to conduct a performance
of his own opera *Ariadne auf Naxos* in Berlin. The Bacchus for this
performance had fallen ill, and a telegram was sent to Dresden:
WE NEED A BACCHUS FOR ARIADNE THE DAY AFTER TO-
MORROW. ANSWER IMMEDIATELY.

"Musically, Bacchus was known as a very demanding role,"
Richard said. "Experts considered it impossible to sing if one hadn't
mastered it entirely. I knew the role only slightly, but agreed to
sing it all the same.

"In Berlin Richard Strauss, who was to conduct the performance himself, said he would go through the most critical sections
with me an hour before the performance, and the night before, I
looked through the piano score.

"After the performance Strauss thanked me for helping out at
such short notice: 'How lucky that you had already studied Bacchus!' he said. 'Where had you sung it before?' 'Nowhere,' I
answered, 'Tonight was the first time.' His mouth gaped wide
open, his eyes flashed angrily, and he turned on me: 'If I had known

that, I would never have conducted the performance myself!'"

However, as a token of gratitude, Strauss presented Richard with a cigar-holder once owned by Richard Wagner, which his widow Diana now owns.

Subconscious into Reality

Richard's Dresden contract expired in 1918, but was renewed for a further five years, during which time he sang seventy roles in operas that included *Carmen, Faust, Cavalleria Rusticana, Don Giovanni, La Bohème, Madame Butterfly* and *The Bartered Bride.* Eugene Tharia wrote of his *La Traviata* in the Dresdner Anzeiger in September 1919: "On the basis of yesterday's performance, Verdi's opera should be called *Alfred Germont* in Dresden, and not *La Traviata,* for in Tauber's warm-blooded, sympathetically thought out performance Germont was decidedly the chief character of the opera, even if Tauber's tenor does not have the melting sweetness for the *dolce* and *dolcissimo* of Verdi's music."

In 1919 Richard agreed to make three guest appearances at the Berlin State Opera and a year later at the Vienna Volksoper he deputized for Alfred Piccaver in *La Bohème* with Lotte Lehmann.

"I remember having trouble with the claque at this performance," Richard recalled. "They had demanded fifty kronen for the performance, which I couldn't afford, and my manager refused to pay.

"'Are you insane?' I exclaimed, 'you will ruin me! You'd better telephone the director, Schalk. Tell him I cannot appear. They will have to find someone else!' The claque had two days in which to organize my failure in Vienna, but my manager promised to put it right on the night of my performance.

"The evening of the performance as I waited to go on I was more depressed than ever at my expected reception. Schalk himself was to conduct that evening, and the house was filled to capacity.

"I sang, and the house remained dead silent. But at that moment it didn't matter, for I was not the celebrated Richard Tauber, but

the poor poet Rodolfo in a Montmartre attic room, in love with
the sweet Mimi, played by Lotte Lehmann. After Mimi's first aria
—frenetic applause. I deceived myself that I wasn't hurt by my
silent reception.

"Then my great aria came, and I sang: '*Und wer seid Ihr?*' A
strange rustle swept through the auditorium and a few seconds
later the frenzy swept through the Wiener Hofoper, so loudly, so
spontaneously, that the Wiener Philharmoniker drew in their
heads to allow the waves of applause to roar unhindered to the
stage.

"After the performance, director Schalk came to my dressing
room with a contract for three more rôles: Pedro in *Tiefland*,
Tamino in *Zauberflöte* and Don Ottavio in *Don Giovanni*.

"Over dinner that evening, I thanked my manager: 'Thank
goodness you managed to get the fifty kronen to the head of the
claque in time,' I said with relief. But he drew from his pocket the
precious fifty kronen which he had folded neatly, ready to press
into the hand of the head of the claque. I didn't understand.

"'At the start of the performance,' he explained, 'I began
pushing my way through to Schostal, the head of the claque, but
it was so crowded that I couldn't reach him by the time your duet
had ended. Then your great aria came and everyone applauded
like mad. When I finally reached him he was so busy applauding
and shouting "Bravo Tauber, Bravo Tauber!" that he didn't
notice me. I finally attracted his attention and he turned on me and
said: "Isn't he marvellous? Why the devil aren't you clapping!"
He then continued applauding like a thing possessed, leading his
followers, their feet stamping on the floor.'

"And with that, my manager returned me the precious fifty
kronen!"

Paternal Pride

Richard returned to Dresden for guest performances and was
invited back to the Vienna State Opera for performances of *La
Traviata, Carmen, Zigeunerbaron* and Hoffman's *Erzählungen*. He

wrote to a friend the following instructions for his comforts, including a request for an amorous assignation:

Dresden,
11th October 1920

I arrive in Vienna on December 8th and shall stay until the 17th. I would be pleased if you could spare some time to see me, and perhaps you would let me know whether you would like to spend a few days with us. Please reserve rooms and a bath at the Regina and make sure the room is centrally heated. I would rather do without a bed than without heating. The room has to be warm, which is very important, and not only for an hour a day, otherwise I shall have to move out and find somewhere else. I would be very happy to have a few pleasant days in Vienna, and perhaps you would reserve a few other things for me. Are you still in contact with the "girls to buy?" If so, please contact the little one (you know the one I mean), and let her know about my arrival. Let me know her address by return.

I shall be singing *la Traviata* on the 9th, *Carmen* on the 11th and 12th, *Zigeunerbaron* on the 16th, and *Erzahlungen* on the 16th. I am looking forward to seeing Vienna again.

I gave two successful performances in Prague. I shall write to Pollak.

Are you able to exhibit pictures of me at first-class venues? If so, let me know and I will let you have some good pictures for publicity purposes.

Please inform me about everything, especially about the hotel.

In old friendship,
Yours,
Richard.

"Daddy is carrying a bundle of your Vienna notices about with him in his breast pocket," Richard's step-brother Otto wrote to him. " 'What do you think about my son Richard's sensational success in Vienna,' he asks everyone who comes near him. 'Just hear what Vienna's tough critics write about him.' And he reads the poor victim your notices. But what is worse is that he has already read everybody every single notice at least twice already, and I fear people are beginning to avoid encounters in case they be exposed to yet another reading!"

"I visited Papa in Chemnitz after my absence in Vienna," Richard said, "and he welcomed me by saying: 'Do you know, Richard, that our relationship has changed completely?' I looked at him in astonishment, 'No Papa, why?' My father smirked to hide his deep inner feeling and replied: 'In the early days, I was generally asked "Herr General Intendant, is this young tenor Tauber your son?" And now I am asked, "Herr General Intendant, are you Richard Tauber's father? Do you realize the difference, Richard?"' And then he smiled happily. He was proud of me.

"He was strangely possessive over me and became jealous of anyone, whether man, woman or object—like my car, for instance—he was desperately jealous of that—and of my hobby, photography—because these things possessed me, and made demands on me and my time."

Richard's goal had been the Vienna State Opera, and now he had certainly arrived. He was to remain under contract for guest appearances for many years. His fame had spread throughout Austria and Germany and his *Don Ottavio* had reached its peak. "Never has Don Ottavio, a figure who usually remains in the background, been received with such a storm of applause, and Don Giovanni himself been overshadowed," a notice read.

Success after success followed. He sang Wilhelm Kienzl's *Evangelimann* at the Vienna State, and received the following letter from Kienzl:

Vienna,
2 Schreigass 6,
11th February 1922

My dear very esteemed artist,
My Wonderful *Evangelimann*,

The overpowering amount of telegrams and letters of congratulations which I received is the reason why I am thanking you so late for your charming and heartfelt warm telegram, but I write

now with double feeling. I read and hear marvellous things about
you and the applause you are so used to hearing. I have the very
pleasant news that you will appear as *Mathias*[1] in a film.[2] Is this
true?

I heard from another source that a *Kuhreiger* film with you as
Primus Thaller is foreseen. This news pleases me very much, and if
you are playing, it must be good.

Will you let me know what is the truth about these rumours or
plans.

With kind regards from both my wife and me,
Yours sincerely,
Doctor Wilhelm Kienzl.

"Whenever I listen to the *Evangelimann* (The Evangelist),"
Richard said, "or take part in it, I think of goulash. After our performance of *Evangelimann* at the Vienna State, Kienzl invited the
artistes to his apartment for a goulash dinner. In Paris you eat at
the Ritz, in London at the Savoy or Claridge's. But the best
cooking I know of is Frau Kienzl's goulash. I think of her goulash
so often. How can one grow so nostalgic for food!"

[1] The role Richard had sung in *Der Evangelimann*.
[2] The film was made, starring Elisabeth Bergner.

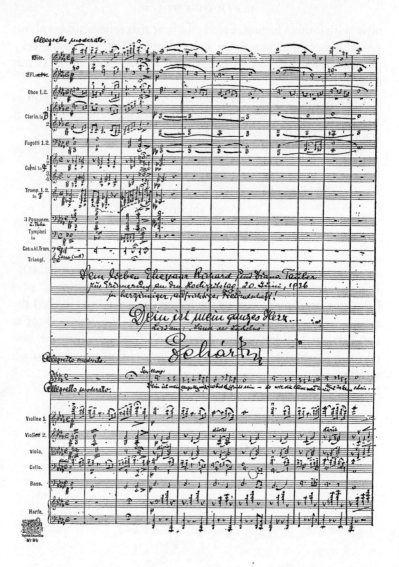

III
THE LAND OF LEHAR

Franz Lehar was born in 1870 of Austro-Hungarian parents. His father's military background as a bandleader in Prague led young Franz into a similar career, he studied the violin and later became Regimental Bandmaster. His early musical training was under Anton Dvořak, who at twenty-five had become conductor of the Neues Deutsches Landestheater, where he encouraged Lehar to compose.

Lehar had composed a handful of reasonably successful operettas by that time, but his first real success came with a commission in 1902 from the Princess Metternich, wife of the Austrian Ambassador in Paris, who asked him to compose a waltz for her Gold and Silver Ball.

The Gold and Silver Waltz spiralled Lehar to international acclaim as the natural successor to Johann Strauss. But it was the success of his *The Merry Widow* at the Theater an der Wien in 1905, with Mizzi Günther and Louise Treumann, that rocketed Lehar's name to unparallelled heights. Productions throughout the world were to follow in twenty-two different languages. Three films were to be made: Von Stroheim's original silent film starring Mae Murray and John Gilbert; the Jeanette MacDonald and Maurice Chevalier version; and finally the one with Lana Turner and Fernando Lamas.

During ninety-three days, between 1910 and 1911, Lehar was to produce three of his most important works, which ran concurrently in Vienna: *The Prince's Child, The Count of Luxembourg* and *Gypsy Love*, between them containing ten of his best marches and twenty-two of his most famous waltzes.

But the assassination of the Archduke Franz Ferdinand precipitated war and imposed silence on Lehar's pen.

He retired to his villa at Ischl, from which he emerged after the war; but he was unable to top his original successes. He enjoyed individual success with his compositions, but the books of the operettas were bad and the runs became shorter and shorter. Although he was at the height of his artistic powers, the Viennese critics neglected him for the new craze of jazz.

However in 1924 his new operetta *Frasquita* opened at the Theater an der Wien. It told the story of the gypsy Frasquita, who lures the good Armand into the labyrinth of her love.

Frasquita was running into trouble, and Richard was called in to the rescue. But he was under contract to the Vienna State Opera, and was only able to take over the rôle months later—much to the chagrin of the State Opera's director, Schalk, who felt Richard was "stepping down" to perform in operetta.

Richard appeared nevertheless, and sang the Serenade *"Hab' ein blaues Himmelbett"* ("Farewell my love, Farewell") for the first time. Audiences flocked to hear him, and the box-office was restored to health. It was to become the first link in a chain of golden melodies Lehar was to compose especially for Richard. This partnership became the hallmark for subsequent Lehar successes.

"I started my guest performance at the Theater an der Wien in Lehar's *Frasquita* in summer 1924," Richard recalled. "It was an extremely hot summer and the theatre was still half empty. A week after I took over the audiences started growing. The houses became better and better. My main song, the Serenade beginning *Schatz ich bitt' Dich, komm heut' Nacht*! was soon sung and played in every cafe, bar and nightclub. Every typist hummed it at her keyboard, every lover crooned it to his sweetheart.

"But opera lovers disapproved of my singing operetta: 'It might not harm your voice,' they said, 'but what about your reputation?' 'It is not worthy of a Wiener Staatsoper artiste,' they cried. But my answer was that a singer did not sing according to his rank, but sang everything that he was capable of singing."

Richard's rescue of Lehar was to lead to success upon success for them both. Their partnership flourished with *Paganini, Friederike,*

Zarevitch, Schön ist die Welt, The Land of Smiles and *Giuditta*—the last Lehar operetta Richard sang and, as a result, the last that Lehar composed. Had it not been for Richard, Lehar might not have been inspired to create so many lovely melodies. The Tauberlied was born and became an essential ingredient of every new Lehar operetta. It was to rocket both singer and composer to unsurpassed operetta heights.

Paganini

In 1924, ill in bed, on the eve of his birthday, Lehar picked up the book of *Paganini*. He was so taken with it that he rose at once and went to his piano. By midnight he had composed the first act— "My birthday gift from dear God," he signed the score.

"During the Salzburg Festival, the Master, Lehar, summoned me to his home in Ischl," Richard continued, "'I have just finished the Tauberlied for *Paganini*,' he announced proudly, 'it is called *"Gern hab' ich die Frau'n geküsst"* ' ('Girls were Made to Love and Kiss')."

But when Paganini opened at the Johann Strauss Theatre in Vienna in 1925, it was without Richard, for he was under contract to sing in Stockholm.

"However I signed a contract with the director, Heinz Saltenburg, of the Deutches Künstler Theatre in Berlin, to appear in fifty performances of *Paganini*, in 1926, for the German première. But when I arrived in Berlin in October 1926, Saltenburg refused to present the operetta. It had failed catastrophically in Vienna, and he believed that because of this it couldn't possibly succeed in Berlin either.

"But Lehar insisted that Saltenburg honour his contract, and the matter was referred to a theatrical court of arbitration. The outcome was that I was to renounce half my fee, Lehar agreed to take a cut in his percentage and the number of performances was reduced to twenty.

"During rehearsals, Lehar and I were subjected to every conceivable indignity. Saltenburg disregarded us completely. Once when he passed me with his nose in the air, I stopped him: "'Tell me', I said, 'what do you intend to do if *Paganini* becomes a great success and the public demand more than twenty performances?'

"Saltenburg looked at me with pity, patted me patronizingly on the shoulder and replied, 'My dear friend, I'll be happy to get through the first night without scandalizing the audience!'

"Saltenburg refused to invite Lehar to conduct, and at the Première of his own operetta the composer and his wife found themselves in a box that Lehar had been compelled to pay for himself. But when after my big song *'Gern hab' ich die Frau'n geküsst'* ('Girls were Made to Love and Kiss'), the audience went wild and shouted for Lehar, Saltenburg changed his tune and took Lehar on stage to receive his ovation.

"Afterwards Lehar said to me with tears in his eyes: 'Do you know, Richard, at that moment I was born an artiste for a second time.'"

After the hundredth performance, Saltenburg insisted on a further two hundred performances with Richard in the title role and Vera Schwarz again as his leading lady, but Richard had other commitments, and could only agree to a further fifty performances. He was now in a position to insist on the terms stipulated in his original agreement in Vienna; and Lehar, too, only agreed to further performances of his work at a *higher* box office percentage than originally agreed.

Richard and Vera Schwarz, who had now become guarantees for the success of every operetta in which they appeared, were equally well received in Lehar's *Zarevitch* the following year at the same theatre.

When criticized for prostituting his operatic voice in operetta, Richard snapped back "I sing Lehar, not operetta!"

"In 1927," Richard said, "I was still under contract to appear as guest artiste in Dresden. I spent my holidays with my mother in Salzburg and sang Lehar's operetta *Zigeunerliebe*. As the audience was to be a very small one, my director proposed going to Ischl to ask Lehar to conduct himself, as an economy.

"Lehar had a charming double-fronted villa on the banks of the River Traun at Bad Ischl, a spa much loved by the old Emperor

Franz Josef. It was here that Lehar had composed over thirty major works, including *The Merry Widow*.

"Convinced that I would succeed in persuading the Master to conduct with the 'power of my charm', I went up to him, bowed, and asked if he would conduct in Salzburg. 'Certainly not. Out of the question. Under no circumstances,' he replied.

"Dejected, I asked whether he would at least autograph a photograph of himself—a small trophy for my nerve!—and he promised to send it to my hotel. We shook hands as though we had been friends for years, and I returned to my hotel, where I eagerly awaited the promised photograph.

"Finally the page-boy brought me a sealed envelope with the photograph, signed: 'Herrn Rudolph Tauber in friendly remembrance.'

"*Rudolph* Tauber! I almost tore it up in rage. I'd been lyrical tenor at the Dresden opera for eight years, sung Lehar's operetta *Paganini* and rescued him from Saltenburg. Yet the amiable Master did not even know that the talented young singer's name was *Richard*!

"When I was the centre of attraction at the Salzburger Festspiele," Richard continued, "my mother, a sweet old woman of nearly eighty, lived in a ground floor flat in Salzburg, in very humble circumstances. My wishes to make her life as simple and agreeable as possible were scorned. I wanted to buy her a small dream villa in the country, but nothing would induce her to leave her little flat, with its old-fashioned plush sofa with crochet-laced panels to protect the arms from wear and tear.

"There was an old plush cloth on the table too, and heavy curtains prevented the daylight she so longed for from filtering into the room. The walls were covered with pictures of me, from ceiling to floor. They were glued on, pinned on or fixed on with nails, staring out from every possible angle. In the centre of the room stood an old-fashioned gramophone with an enormous horn. She would sit with her ear pressed to it for hours on end, listening to one after the other of the dozens of my recordings that she owned.

"My mother's affections for me was as great as my father's, but it showed itself in different ways. Even at her age she still looked upon me as her little boy. Although she was thrilled by my fame, it didn't impress her in the least.

"I'd been singing Tamino in *Zauberflöte* and Don Ottavio at the Salzburg Festival, and finding spare time one morning, I hurried along to see my mother, whom I found in the kitchen, preparing lunch. She was busily stirring a saucepan of stew on the stove, and when I greeted her, she said without looking up: 'I'm glad you've come, Richard. Please run along to the grocer and fetch a half a litre of vinegar. Tell them to put it on my account.'

"With that, she handed me an empty bottle, and I, the star of the Festival, went to the grocer's in a daze. I made my way through the chattering housewives and like a little boy asked for the half litre of vinegar!

"She died at the age of ninety-two in 1938, but war prevented me from being at her deathbed or her graveside. I couldn't be near her in her last hour. Nor could I close my father's eyes when he died in Switzerland four years after my mother died."

IV
LIEDER

The singing of German Lieder demands a high degree of poetic and artistic sensibility, as well as a finely controlled technique that is capable of a wide range of power and expressiveness. Richard's voice was always outstandingly natural and unaffected when he sang Lieder.

Because of the richness and melting sweetness of his voice, and his manner of refining simple, plain language, Richard was to become an acknowledged interpreter of the German folksong. The *Winterreise Cycle* (Winter Journey) has seldom been sung in a simpler and more beautiful way. For the most charming of the folk songs, including *Du, du liegst mir im Herzen* and *Kommt a Vogerl geflogen*, he was accompanied on record by Mischa Spoliansky.

Spoliansky, who was born in Bialistock, in Tzarist Russia, had grown up in a musical environment. His father was an opera singer, his brother a cellist and his sister a concert pianist. He had his first piano lesson at five. By the time he was in his early twenties, he was introduced in Berlin, to the great theatre producer Max Reinhardt, who commissioned him to compose the music for his production of Somerset Maugham's *Home and Beauty*. This proved such a success that it led to another commission—this time for Marlene Dietrich, in 1928, for whom he composed a musical comedy, *Es Liegt in der Luft* (It's in the Air), which was to be the start of Dietrich's international recognition in this field.

Spoliansky's songs were new and original combining wit with feeling in a manner so spirited and elegant that they provided Berlin with a wholly novel experience. "Mischa Spoliansky's music and instrumentation top anything heard in Berlin in the last few years in richness of idea, verve and elegance," said one commentator. The Berliner Boersenkurier wrote of *It's in the Air*: "This is perfection. Spoliansky's music is in a class by itself. An individual spirit and delicacy which lies in the plane of great music. A flowering of ideas. Incredible nobility, colour, delicate hues . . . dynamite."

Success followed success until *Tell me Tonight*, a Jan Kiepura film that brought him to London, where he has lived ever since as one of our most respected film composers. He has composed for dozens of films, including *King Solomon's Mines*, *Sanders of the River*, *The Happiest Days of Your Life*, *The Man who Could Work Miracles*, *Duel in the Jungle* and *North West Frontier*.

"I accompanied Richard in Berlin in 1925," Spoliansky told me from the drawing room of his Mount Street home. "We recorded Schubert's *Winterreise* Cycle and an album of folk songs which were highly regarded by the critics at the time, and have become collectors' items.

"Unfortunately, recording techniques in those days were not up to the standard of today's, and they don't stand up well to reproduction.

"We completed the recording of the folk songs in one morning with only a coffee break in between—which, you must admit, was remarkable.

"Richard was an extremely likeable person with a wonderful sense of humour. He had a sort of boyish exhuberance, punning continuously.

"I remember going to rehearsal at the Opera in Dresden, where the resident tenor was just about to hit the high C when fear overtook him and he stopped abruptly. Richard's voice rang out from the back of the stalls, filling in the missing note—and we all applauded like mad!

"His voice was not a powerful one, but it had a special lyrical quality which, coupled with his own kind of interpretation, created a personal style.

"He had remarkable warmth and was always generous in his appreciation of other musicians. He was in love, not so much with singing, as with music—a thoroughly trained musician first, and a singer second."

Turandot

A year later, in 1926, the critics who had condemned Richard for singing in operetta, praised him for his guest appearance in Dresden. The German Première of Puccini's unfinished opera *Turandot* was in preparation when the tenor, Curt Taucher, was taken ill, and Richard was asked to take over the new role at three days' notice. He burned the midnight oil and sang, with the American soprano Anne Roselle in the name part.

Turandot had its German Première on July 4th 1926 and was a great success. No opera had been so gorgeously staged since the Great War, and audiences who saw both original productions claimed that it outdid the La Scala Milan's original production. Anne Roselle, who won extraordinary praise, embodied all the requirements of a model Turandot with a voice of rare carrying power and brilliance. Although her success was tremendous, it was Richard who received the finest notice: "Among the soloists Richard Tauber without doubt earned first place. He learned the part in three days; a feat of bravery unprecedented in the annals of opera. In spite of this last minute take-over he sang the part excellently, with complete comprehension of its musical and dramatic possibilities. He appeared young and attractive, a genuine Prince. He sang with just the right mixture of poetical ardour and masterly Italian *cantilena*. In short, his portrayal was almost perfection."

With this production, Dresden had certainly re-established a renown that had been waning as a result of the aftermath of the Great War. The production was the turning point in the opera's fortunes.

Nuptials Destined for Disaster

The following year, Richard married opera singer Carlotta Vanconti. This was due indirectly to Lea Seidl, the scintillating Austrian singing star, who was later to appear in England in many successes, including Lehar's *Friederike* and Robert Stolz's *White Horse Inn*.

"I was in Vienna doing three weeks as guest artiste in Emmerich Kálmán's *Countess Maritza,*" said Lea Seidl, who has lived in London since before the war. "The day I returned to Berlin, Richard came to see the show in Vienna, and my understudy, Carlotta Vanconti, was on.

" 'This is very annoying!' Richard said to the producer, who was with him in the box. 'Oh, do be kind to the understudy,' the producer replied. 'She is so proud. She thinks that you came specially to hear *her* performance.'

"So Richard, his usual friendly self, went backstage to congratulate her after the performance, and when he met her it was love at first sight.

"Later, when they were doing a show together, the conductor, who was rather short, peeped through the keyhole while they were rehearsing. He saw Richard desperately trying to woo her, and Carlotta replying: 'No, no, Richard. I'm not in the mood. I'm too worried about my jewellery. I've had to pawn it, and I simply don't have the money to redeem it.'

" 'Don't you worry about that,' he heard Richard say, 'I'll get it out for you.' And it cost him thousands of marks—more than he had bargained for. But that was Richard all over!

"Soon after that they married, and unfortunately she then tried to give him singing lessons—and I think that *that* killed the marriage!"

The marriage lasted only a year—not only because Carlotta, who considered herself a greater star, had insisted on becoming Richard's singing teacher, but because she had asked him for his written permission to sleep with another man. She used their marital problems as a lever to get Richard's signature, but since she was already unfaithful to him he saw little point in signing. She then threatened to go to the national press with intimate details of their marriage—details that might damage Richard's masculine image and harm his romantic appeal. He signed.

Divorce proceedings began, but they were later to have repercussions in the law courts, when Vanconti demanded more and more money to keep quiet.

V
DEATH'S STRANGE TIMBRE

On October 4th 1928, the world première of Lehar's *Friederike* took place at the Metropol Theatre in Berlin, with the brilliant Kathé Dorsch in the name part and Richard as Goethe.

"To be sung to by Richard Tauber and be paid for it too is simply glorious!" Kathé Dorsch said at the time.

There had been criticism about making Germany's leading poet the subject of an operetta, but it proved a great success and played to sold-out houses. Richard scored another hit with his Tauberlied 'O *Mädchen, mein Mädchen*' ('O Maiden, my Maiden').

But sitting in the audience was one of Germany's famous actresses, and she did not care for him in the role in the slightest.

Elisabeth Bergner

Born in Vienna in 1900, Elisabeth Bergner made her first appearance in Berlin at the Deutsches Volkstheater under Max Reinhardt, playing Katherina in *The Taming of the Shrew*, the Queen in *Richard II* and Rosalind in *As you Like It*. In 1924 her St Joan earned her an international reputation. Subsequently she became known in England, particularly for her memorable stage performance in *Escape Me Never*, presented by C. B. Cochran in 1933, and in *The Boy David*, specially written for her by Sir James Barrie in 1936—the last play he wrote.

She was the first actress to receive the Schiller Prize (in 1963) for *The Mad Woman of Chaillot*. Her film career had begun in 1923 with *Der Evangelimann*, in which Richard had scored such a success at the Vienna State Opera, and she was to go from one film success to another—among them *Catherine the Great* and *Dreaming Lips*, both directed by her husband, Dr Paul Czinner.

When she was filming *Dreaming Lips* at Denham before the war, the only stage to be shrouded in secrecy, with shooting taking place behind locked doors, was Bergner's. Marlene Dietrich was then filming *Knight Without Armour* with Robert Donat and John Clements for London Film Productions on the next stage.

Bergner was the first star in England known to begin filming as late as twelve noon, a civilized habit she had cultivated in European film studios.

"I first heard Tauber sing Goethe," said Elisabeth Bergner, who has miraculously retained her youthful beauty and exquisite style. She and her husband have lived in London's Eaton Square since the war, and it was from there that she told me about her first encounter with Richard. "I thought he was just a musical comedy clown who could sing. I had gone to hear an actress whom I loved very much—Kathé Dorsch—playing Friederike. Now she didn't offend me at all in that part, but he did. It was awful. I think I left before the end. But then, about a year or so later, I went to the opera to hear *Don Giovanni* because there was a new Don whom we were all talking about—Michael Bohnen. But what I really heard and saw was Tauber singing Ottavio. It was fortunate for me that I was in a box by myself because I went out of my mind, I was so shaken, and I was so humbled by my first rejection of such an enormous artiste. Well, afterwards, I only went to hear Tauber for his own sake."

Close to Death

It was while he was singing Goethe in *Friederike* that an attack of arthritis, the result of a bitter winter that had frozen the Rhine, gave rise to concern about Richard's future. He was unable to go on, and performances were cancelled. Newspapers had reported that his career had come to an end; that he would never sing again. Unable to move, he was taken by ambulance to the station, where he left for the Slovakian Spa at Pistyan. Here he was treated by immersion in hot sulphuric mud, and months later he was able to return to Vienna for the world Première of *The Land of Smiles*.

"I was indeed very close to death," Richard said. "It was in January 1929 that I suddenly fell seriously ill. Somehow the closeness to death, and the recovery from being so near to it seemed to have some effect on my voice. Perhaps in those dying months death had played its violin with notes heard only by me in my sleepless, painful nights and taught me how to sing, for on my recovery my voice developed a warm sound, the lack of which had previously deprived it of perfection.

"It happened when I was in Hanover, shortly before the end of the *Friederike* tour. I had developed a sore throat and asked for the hotel doctor. He was a friendly, elderly man. He examined me, and with the use of cotton-wool extracted two blockages which had lodged in my throat. I felt better at once and prepared to leave for the evening concert performance. But my manager insisted that I wasn't up to it, and cancelled the performance.

"I left immediately by car for Berlin, where I had an apartment at the Hotel Adlon. I thought the car journey accounted for my extreme fatigue, but my secretary Otto insisted that I go to bed at once. I was irritable and barked at him: 'I employ you as my secretary, and not as my nurse. If I wanted a nurse I would find a pretty teenager! Now leave me alone!'

"I went to bed, and just as I dropped off, the telephone rang. It was my father, calling from Chemnitz. He had heard of the concert cancellation in Hanover and was worried. I grumbled about Otto's fuss over me, and he seemed delighted in my complaining, for he was insanely jealous of anyone who tried to take care of me.

"When I tried to replace the telephone receiver I was unable to move my arm—but I put this down to my tiredness and thought no more of it. The following morning I still felt exhausted, but otherwise quite well and fit. I checked my voice, and it seemed all right too.

"So I dressed, ordered a car, and went to the AFA studio where Henny Porten was filming.

"Henny and her husband were my truest and most sincere

friends. When I saw them that day in Berlin I didn't realise that a few days later this friendship would be put to the severest test and that they would emerge as kind and noble as I had suspected they would.

"At the studio we chatted happily and lunched in the canteen, discussing plans for the future.

"But after my day off, I had to return to work. To opera performances, concerts, and recording sessions. I remember sitting on a low chair at a recording session and finding that my legs had gone dead as far up as the knee. I couldn't stand up. My legs had turned to lead, and I could barely drag myself to my feet and stagger to the car where my secretary was waiting for me.

"He took me back to the hotel and put me to bed. I developed a terrible headache and my temperature began to soar. The elderly hotel doctor was called again, but he said it was only a cold and that a hot bath and bed would help to sweat it out.

"I woke in the middle of the night. I could move neither my legs nor my arms. And I couldn't turn over. And then I thought, 'what of my voice—what if I can't sing either?' The panic drove me mad, and I called out: 'Otto! Come quickly!' At least I knew my voice was still there.

"Otto tried to move my arms and legs, and I screamed with pain. The joints were swollen and I couldn't move. But that was only the start.

"For four months I was to remain in bed, literally packed in cotton wool. I had lived for thirty-seven years without serious illness and now it seemed to be catching up on me in one bitter attack. Doctors and specialists came to my bedside, but were unable to help.

"Otto refused to allow me to be taken to hospital and nursed me himself. I was worried about money. As I was out of work there was no income, and my expenses and doctors' bills were soaring. I had never been one to save, so there was nothing put by.

"The weeks came and went. A few people visited me out of sympathy; most out of business interest; and others out of curiosity, to see the breathing mummified famous tenor packed in cotton wool.

"Journalists called and their headlines later read: 'Richard Tauber's life threatened!' 'Tauber will never appear on stage again!'

"On reading their reports, Alfred Rotter director of the Berliner Metropoltheater, visited me to say that if the newspapers were correct my existing *Friederike* contract would have to be cancelled.

"And then, quiet reigned. Telephone calls from Vienna, Paris and London came to a halt. It seemed that everyone was waiting for the news of my death.

"I found my real friends; the ones who not only gave helpful, encouraging advice, but gave me a reason to fight on and win through. Henny Porten and her husband Dr Kaufmann. Marlene Dietrich, this very kind and dear friend, although she was on the other side of the Atlantic, had assured me of all financial help if I needed it. Kammersängerin Vera Schwarz, actress Agnes von Esterhazy and singer Edi Lichtenstein stayed with me for hours on end, cheering me up, comforting me in every possible way.

"And then came the endless nights with unbearable pain, where only morphine could help. I was to become so used to that malicious consoler that I couldn't live without it.

" 'If only I could recover enough to sit in a wheelchair,' I said to my secretary, 'and move my hands, then perhaps I could record again—or at least teach singing.' But all other performing was over; opera, concerts . . . everything was gone. I developed a crying fit, and Otto shook me until I fell asleep with exhaustion.

"Papa often came to visit me, but he made me so nervous with his helpless despair that I asked him not to come again, to telephone from Chemnitz instead.

"It was a great comfort when Lehar came to see me to discuss turning his *Gelbe Jacke* (The Yellow Jacket) into an operetta to be called *Das Land des Lächelns* (The Land of Smiles.) For hours he studied the score with me and contributed greatly to my physical recovery, although it must have begun already, for otherwise I wouldn't have had the strength to be interested in the work.

"After an examination, the doctor suggested I go to Bad Pistyan, the only possible hope of a cure for me. So I was taken there by car, and carried on a stretcher.

"Marlene Dietrich and Henny Porten were at the station to say good-bye, and there were hundreds of people there—but not to see *me* off to recovery. Wherever Dietrich and Porten went, crowds gathered in abundance.

"At Pistyan, the exhausting journey along the road to recovery began—I was immersed in hot sulphuric mud baths daily.

"One night I awoke. Something was tickling my nose. It was a fly. Still half asleep, I lifted my arm and shoo'd it away. I lay still in sublime shock. I had moved my arm! I could move! I could move my right arm quite well, and the left only a bit—but it *did* move! I could have kissed the friendly fly, who had flown from me by now—I laughed and cried with joy till the early morning, then fell into a deep, strengthening sleep.

"I contacted my friends. They came. I tried my voice and heard in it something strange and new. I sang *mezza voce* in my hotel room at Bad Pistyan for my friends—Henny Porten and her husband, and the film actress Hanni Weisse. Henny burst into tears of happiness. I wondered what it was in my voice that was strange and new. Before, my voice had shown my unconcerned youth, happiness and fervour, and perhaps even sensuality, but now that I had stared into the eyes of death for nights on end, deep grief and renunciation, happiness and gratitude melted it to a strange timbre which I was never to lose.

"Later, at a concert at the Albert Hall in London in 1934, King George V said to me: 'You don't sing with your throat, but with your heart.' I could only stammer back: 'Your Majesty, you have summed up in a few words the highest aim of every singer!'

Dutch Treat

"In July 1929 I sang and played young Goethe in Lehar's *Friederike* in Amsterdam; the Amsterdam *Telegraaf* wrote: '*Oh Mädchen, mein Mädchen* . . . ! Half Amsterdam was in the theatre! And in that heat! Even though we had heard it all day long from the milkman whistling it on the street, the postman humming it . . . well, the first '*M*' of this '*Madchen*'—you simply must hear it sung by Richard Tauber, with his vibrating consonants, his caressing tone, his warmth, his charm—it is unique! Tauber sang it again, the audience was spellbound. Yet again he sang it, and the audience went wild. And then Tauber started for the fourth time!'

"Needless to say, Papa carried these notices around for weeks and read them to everyone he met!"

Success and Rejection

Franz Lehar had composed *The Land of Smiles*, then called *The Yellow Jacket*, years before, when it had received bad notices and failed to run. Inspired by the success of *Madame Butterfly* and *The Geisha*, he had decided to try his hand at an operetta with an oriental setting, but the story had lacked conviction and the score, although containing some beautiful melodies, had failed to please the audiences. He decided to rewrite it for Richard, but the Pistyan excursion seemed to stand in the way. Would Richard ever be well enough again to sing?

Then Lehar had a brilliant inspiration. Richard could play a Chinaman; hiding his arthritic wrists beneath kimono sleeves and using the characteristic stage pseudo-Chinese walk to conceal the limp in his lame left leg.

But the score still lacked the Tauberlied which audiences had come to expect. Providence then played its usual rôle in Richard's career, for whilst idly glancing through some of Lehar's old manuscripts at Bad Ischl he came across a tune that he liked. He sat down at the piano with the music and played it, humming the melody, and before long decided that this piece of music dug up from the past, 'You Are my Heart's Delight', would become the Tauberlied for *The Land of Smiles*.

The Land of Smiles is set in Vienna, and tells of how Lisa, a General's daughter, becomes infatuated with a Chinese prince. But Prince Sou-chong (Richard) leaves for China the following day, and Lisa decides to ditch her young man, Captain Gustav von Ploetz, to follow the prince to China. They meet up and marry, but "a Mandarin cannot mate with a white woman", and arrangements have been made for Sou-chong to marry four Manchu maidens in order to continue the dynasty. Sou-chong makes it clear that he loves his European wife and that these marriages shall be marriages in name only, and Lisa and Sou-chong sing the passionate duet 'Love, what has given you this magic power?'

Meanwhile Sou-chong has been told that he has to go through with the four marriages, but he will not consent to renouncing Lisa. Unable to accept the situation, Lisa runs away, and Sou-chong sings 'You are my Heart's Delight'.

Lisa turns to her first love, Gustav, and Sou-chong declares his love for Lisa to be strong enough for him to give her what she desires—her freedom.

The world Première of *The Land of Smiles* took place at the Metropol in Berlin on October 10th 1929, with Richard, Vera Schwarz and Hella Kürty in the leading parts. It was Lehar's 60th birthday, and he himself conducted.

Meanwhile Lehar was preparing his next operetta, *Schön ist die Welt* (*Beautiful World*). He had rewritten it from another unsuccessful operetta, *Endlich Allein* (*Alone at Last*), which had been performed at the Theater an der Wien in 1914, but now, as in the case of *The Land of Smiles*, a hit song for Richard was essential and this was found in '*Liebste glaub' an mich*' ('Dearest, trust in me').

The reception of *Schön ist die Welt* in December 1930 at the Metropol was the antithesis of that given to *The Land of Smiles*, even though Richard's leading lady was the Hungarian opera star Gitta Alpar.

The critics vied with each other in the praise of the leading artists—"Tauber is a god of song," "Gitta Alpar is sensational," "Richard Tauber and Gitta Alpar, two singers of highest perfection, both incredibly musical and possessors of wonderful voices" . . . but the show flopped.

Alfred and Fritz Rotter, Berlin's foremost impressario/theatre owners had produced three of Richard's successes—*Friederike, The Land of Smiles* and now *Schön ist die Welt*. After the opening of the last operetta, Alfred Rotter wrote to Richard in verse:

> Three times we have made it together,
> Three times you have sung with success.

Again we have done it,
There is no gap in the continuity of our plays
From *Friederike* to *The Land of Smiles*,
We walk together hand in hand
Hoping that our future will remain together,
And our slogan after this success is *Schön ist die Welt!*

But catastrophe was near for the Rotter brothers. The failure of
Paul Abraham's *Bal im Savoy* (*Ball at the Savoy*), which the brothers
had presented in Berlin, led to financial disaster. Bernard Grun
explains what happened in his biography of Franz Lehar, *Gold and
Silver*, published by W. H. Allen:

"Christmas was celebrated at their Grunewald villa, in the
middle of January. Even before an investigation of their accounts
could throw light on the business affairs of their theatrical com-
bine, the brothers lost their heads and fled to Lichtenstein.

"A few weeks later they became victims of their indestructible
stage enthusiasm. A resident who had hobnobbed with them
talked about a farmer's boy in the neighbourhood with an un-
usually fine tenor voice, just waiting to be discovered. Unable to
resist the temptation of giving him an audition, Alfred, his wife
and brother, got into the man's car on the morning of 5th April
1933. When they realized it was a kidnapping coup organized by
a Gestapo spy, they tried to jump out of the vehicle as it raced
towards Germany. Alfred and his wife were killed on the spot,
Fritz managed to escape and struggle through to Paris."

Late in 1930 Richard made his film debut in *Das Dirnenlied*,
later retitled *Ich glaub' nicht mehr an eine Frau*, for which he himself
wrote the title song, 'I'll never believe in a woman again'. His
leading lady was the German actress Maria Solveig. Still slightly
crippled from his illness, he found filming gave him physical
relief from the demands of the stage.

He formed his own film company to make *Das Lockende Ziel*;
the English and French versions were called respectively *The End
of the Rainbow* and *La Marche à la Gloire*; his co-star was the attractive Lucie Englisch. His third film, a version of *The Land of Smiles*,
was altered to make a double bill, in which he played a Prince

being entertained with a performance of a famous operetta in which he also appeared.

Then came *Die grosse Attraktion* (*The Great Attraction*) and finally *Wie werde ich reich und glucklich* (*How to Become Rich and Happy*), both of which were failures, with the result that the film company collapsed, and Richard lost thousands.

The time now came to find fame further afield; but before he left for England and America he had sung in opera and operetta with leading ladies who included Lotte Lehmann, Elizabeth Schumann, Gitta Alpar, Maria Jeritza, Fritzi Massary, Anny Ahlers, Rita Georg, Vera Schwarz and Elizabeth Rethberg.

In 1931 Stanley H. Scott presented *The Land of Smiles* at the Drury Lane Theatre and Richard was paid a reputed £1,500 a week, a figure few stars command today, forty years later. He received the following letter of agreement from Stanley Scott when he returned to play the same role at the Dominion Theatre the following year, at a reduced fee:

Stanley Scott.   His Majesty's Theatre,
                                                                            Haymarket, S.W.1.
                                                                            9th June 1932

Dear Mr Tauber,

I confirm that you will receive £900 (nine hundred pounds) for the seven performances during the week ending 11th June.

You are to receive one hundred pounds (£100) for the extra matinée at Golders Green, over and above the amount due to you for that week. This sum to be paid at the end of the first weeks run at the Dominion Theatre.

Yours sincerely,
Stanley Scott.

The Drury Lane curtain rose in May 1931 with Renee Bullard playing the Vera Schwarz role, and Hella Kürty the part she had created in Germany.

The notices were mixed. According to one of them: "His

wonderful singing roused the audience to a rare pitch of enthusiasm and the scene at the close was, I should think, unprecedented for any musical play and Herr Tauber repeats his famous second-act air 'You are my Heart's Delight' some six times with the most generous complaisance, being obviously willing to oblige till all the seas gang dry or the applause dries up, whichever should be the remoter event. But would it not add to the enjoyment of the evening if this fine singer would consider desisting from this iteration and give us some snatch of Mozart or Schubert, or anything by which we could better judge his quality, since the present piece allows him to touch no note save that of a rather turgid melody."

Whether the cause was notices of this sort, homesickness or the throat trouble of which he was complaining, Richard missed a number of performances and returned to Vienna for treatment, his stand-in, Robert Naylor, taking over the rôle. Richard came back from Vienna with his throat cured, and resumed the role, but in a matter of weeks the show came off, with a loss of thousands to the backers.

Richard then signed a contract for an American concert tour, during the course of which his notices were some of the finest he had ever had. His American programme included an aria from *Joseph in Egypt*, songs from Schumann's *Dichterliebe* and a selection from Lehar's operettas. The American enthusiasm and applause was tremendous. He had scored a triumph.

"Richard Tauber's American debut last night at the Town Hall," the *New York Times* reported, "was the occasion of immense enthusiasm. The personality, the excellent showmanship, the frank and communicative temperament of the singer grew upon the audience. He is born not only with a voice, but with a gift for song. Vocal grace and charm are his natural attributes."

But the English press were not quite so kind when he came back to England. He had returned for concerts in the provinces, and for a Sunday Concert at the Albert Hall on 6th December 1931. He was looking forward to the great event, but once again he developed throat trouble and the performance had to be cancelled on the actual day. The disappointed audience, who could not be notified in time to prevent their arrival, were turned away at the doors.

Richard was spotted passing the Albert Hall in a taxi by a newspaperman, and he was reported to have been seen in a cinema the same evening. For a time he became unpopular with the British public, who considered him unreliable, particularly in view of the disappointment over *The Land of Smiles*, but his doctor has records to prove that the throat trouble was genuine.

However, the English public would neither forgive nor forget, and it was to take him seven years to achieve an invitation to sing *The Magic Flute*, *Don Giovanni* and *The Bartered Bride* at the Royal Opera House, Covent Garden.

But there was the world of British feature films at his feet— successes like *Blossom Time*, *Pagliacci*, *Heart's Desire* and *Land Without Music* were around the corner . . .

PART TWO

The Second Era
1931–1938

VI
WIND OF FEAR

After the Albert Hall disappointment, Richard returned to Berlin for a season at the Metropol of *Das Lied der Liebe* (*The Song of Love*), an operetta compiled by Erich Wolfgang Korngold from existing scores and newly discovered manuscripts by the two Johann Strausses. Productions such as *Waltzes of Vienna* and *The Great Waltz*, containing much of the same music by the Strausses, but with different stories, were to be presented by numerous companies throughout the world in the subsequent forty years but this, the original production, was presented by Alfred and Fritz Rotter, who had fallen out with Lehar. Richard was under contract to the brothers, however, and although his loyalties were with his old friend Lehar, he was advised to honour his contract.

Das Lied der Liebe opened at Christmas 1932 and Richard's first song was 'Tales from the Vienna Woods'. From the moment that he sang it the operetta was assured a run until the following Easter. His leading lady was the beautiful Anny Ahlers, whose career was to end so tragically years later when, as the result of a broken love affair, she threw herself to her death from a Harley Street building.

In May 1932 Richard returned to England for a new production of *The Land of Smiles*, which opened at the Streatham Hill Theatre and then transferred first to Golders Green and later to the Dominion in the West End, with the English opera singer Josie Fearon as his leading lady. But receipts fell, no doubt due to the public believing it to be a film—the Dominion had been known as a cinema until then—and also possibly to loss of faith in Richard's reliability.

Richard's old friend Heinrich Hensel had ideas for a season the following year:

Heinrich Hensel,
    Kammersänger

Hamburg.
Schwanenwik 35,
24 November 1932

Dear Richard,

I have rented the Stadtstheater here for six weeks in the summer of 1933. Shall we do a season of operetta here together? It may mean big business! Make me a proposition. I have the theatre with scenery at my disposal. It would be wonderful if you, my old friend, would find some means of realising this plan. There are no risks as I have the theatre agreement for 35% to 40% less than anyone else pays.

I hope that you are well and happy,

> Your old friend,
> Heinrich.

But Richard wrote back declining the offer, as he was negotiating with the Rotter brothers for performances of *Das Dreimäderlhaus* (*Lilac Time*) in Dresden and the Hague.

The brothers wrote to him two days later:

Rotter.

Berlin—Grunewald, 26 November 1932.
Kunz Buntschuhstr 16–18.

Dear Richard,

I received your telegram. I will give Kochner[1] the first half of December off. I suggest you sing *Dreimäderlhaus* at Christmas in Berlin instead of in Dresden. We could perform it the whole of January, perhaps even longer. Also, a plan has been suggested to perform *The Last Waltz* with you, and maybe Mara[2] over Christmas. In case you cannot fulfil the engagement in Berlin, the Dresden date is definite.

What do you think of the Grosses Schauspielhause (theatre)?

[1] Austrian actor Walter Kochner, who played comedy leads.
[2] Mara Losseff.

Reinhardt has given us excellent terms and we really cannot refuse.

Generally speaking the Deutsches Künstlertheater is a very good choice, and all the productions are proving successful. No doubt you heard of our success with *Konstantin*. We have hired the theatre for a few years. All our Premières are very interesting and, as far as we can judge, will be great hits. We hope for great success with the Abraham operetta[1] with Gitta Alpar. Also Mosheim appears in *Madame Favart* by Offenbach, with Max Hansen starring.

I hope to receive your answer about Berlin as soon as possible.

With best wishes,
Alfred.

Richard returned to Berlin in December 1932 for the new operetta *Frühlingsstürme*, by Josef Weinberger, who was best known for his opera *Schwanda the Bagpiper*. His leading lady was Jarmila Novotna, who had earlier proved a sensational success in Reinhardt's production of Offenbach's *La Belle Hélène*.

But Hitler was inflaming the eight million unemployed in Germany, and Jewish artistes began leaving the country. Richard being non-political, was set upon staying, until on leaving his hotel one night he was assaulted by uniformed rowdies. He now decided to leave, and embarked on a tour of Austria and Switzerland with the Vienna company of *Dreimäderlhaus*. Tours of Sweden and Belgium ended in Holland, where he assembled a new *Dreimäderlhaus* company, which proved so successful that it transferred to London's Aldwych Theatre as *Lilac Time*. This life story of Franz Schubert brought an offer from British International Pictures for Richard to make the film version, called *Blossom Time*, released by MGM in America as *April Romance*, with Jane Baxter, Carl Esmond, Athene Seyler, Paul Graetz and Marguerite Allan in other leading rôles.

Blossom Time was set in Vienna in 1820 and told of Schubert's love for Vicki, the daughter of a dancing master and sweetheart of

[1] *Bal im Savoy*, which was to cause the brothers financial disaster, precipitate their flight from Germany, and lead to Alfred Rotter's untimely death.

a soldier. Schubert sells his piano to buy a dress for Vicki, but she believes it to be a present from her soldier. When Schubert learns that Vicki expects to marry her soldier, he searches the city for him, finds him in a public house, demands to know his intentions, and is thrown out.

Later the soldier apologizes and tells him he would marry Vicki if the Duchess (played by Athene Seyler) had not planned another match for him. Schubert intervenes, obtains her consent, gives the young people his blessing and buries his sorrow in his music, singing 'Love Lost Forever' with the choir at the wedding ceremony.

Jane Baxter

"It was a bit much, Schubert singing 'Love Lost Forever' at my wedding, wasn't it!" Jane Baxter laughed when she told me during her filmed tribute to Richard, about filming *Blossom Time* with him, "When you think it was supposed to have been love sanctified! But it was very romantic all the same, and I loved making the film."

Jane Baxter and her husband, businessman Arthur Montgomery, live in a charming house in Wimbledon. She spoke of her film with Richard in her garden, where forsythia and apple-blossom were in full bloom:

"Of course it was a great thrill for me, early in my career, playing opposite Richard," she said. "It was a lovely experience working with him. He had this exuberant personality and tremendous vitality. He seemed to fill the whole studio with his vitality; like a great shining sun. He was very sympathetic and kind; it was really my happiest film!

"I remember one rather anguished afternoon. There was a scene in which I had to cry and we'd rehearsed it. Paul Stein, the director, told me to take a few minutes to get into the mood of the scene, so I wandered off hopefully into a dark corner, and thought of all the saddest things I could. But the harder I tried, the drier-eyed I became. I was absolutely hopeless. I couldn't produce a tear! So after a little while Paul Stein got rather fed up and called to the make-up man: 'Harry, go and get the glycerine.' I felt awful, absolutely ashamed. I was really feeling the lowest form of life and then Richard said to me ruefully, 'Jane, I thought you were an *actress*,' and I burst into tears! Everyone was delighted, including me! I was very grateful to him!"

However, the German public were never to see *Blossom Time*. Hitler had banned it in January 1935 on the grounds that Richard was an immigrant and did not fulfil the necessary conditions for foreign films in Germany. The truth was that Richard, an Austrian by birth, had Jewish blood, so that the German censor would not even view *Blossom Time*.

"When we'd finished the studio filming," Jane Baxter continued, "we had four days location filming in Vienna. It was lovely. I'd never been there before, and it was June. We were working all day, and when Richard finished filming for the day, he sang in *Giuditta* at the opera House. I was very lucky because the first night I heard Lotte Lehmann in *Rosenkavalier*, and the second night in *Fidelio*. The third night it was Richard and Novotna in *Giuditta*. It was lovely; he was singing so beautifully; it was a heavenly experience."

Giuditta

Giuditta has a colourful if finally unsatisfactory plot about a birdcage-seller's wife who deserts her husband to follow a soldier, and ends up loveless and disillusioned as a nightclub dancer. The music plays a more than usually prominent part, going further than previous Lehar works in its preludes and intermezzos. Giuditta's most famous song, '*Meine Lippen, sie Küssen so heiss*' occurs at the end when Giuditta is discovered in a shady nightclub in North Africa. But although *Giuditta* is strictly dramatic, the old Lehar strain of sentimentality still imbues both melodies and story.

The première took place in 1934, with seats treble the usual price.

"It was quite an historic occasion," Sir David Webster remembered, "because it was the first time in the history of the Vienna Opera that an operetta was performed at the State Opera

House. This operetta was a typical Lehar piece, full of charm, full of lyricism, with a trifle of sentiment here and there, and Tauber was extremely well matched by Novotna, who was one of the most delightful sopranos in the Viennese theatre. The two of them had an enormous success both in Vienna and Berlin, and there's no doubt that this very beautiful and extremely lyrical piece added greatly to his fame.

"I heard a performance of *Giuditta*, and it endeared itself to me with enormous clarity of feeling and charm. Novotna lives in America these days; she was a very beautiful girl, with such a lovely voice.

The Singing Dream

After *Giuditta*, rehearsals for Richard's own operetta *Der Singende Traum* (*The Singing Dream*) began. Richard had composed the music of the Svengali-type story for the singer Mara Losseff, whom he had met through his close friend Marlene Dietrich. But now he had fallen in love with Mara who had Dietrich's style, elegance and beauty.

Mara Losseff, a Russian born in Vladivostok, had fled to Japan at the outbreak of the Revolution. At the age of seven she was sent to a convent, where she remained until her family moved to Germany. Having finished her education in Berlin, she was drawn to the stage. She joined the Nelson Revue, one of the most successful productions of its kind, and soon attracted attention both by her singing and her looks.

She created the rôle of Sonja in *The Singing Dream*, and turned out to be the biggest surprise of the première. She possessed beauty of voice, personal beauty and great charm, the ideal and all-too-rare combination for a light opera *prima donna*. She had fallen deeply in love with her leading man, Richard, and it was rumoured that they would marry.

But she was to have a pathetic end. In real life, too, Richard was to have a Svengali effect on her, and like Trilby she could only really sing under his influence. When he was away from her, she drank. And being Russian, she drank heavily.

She later co-starred with Jack Buchanan in his film *The Sky's the Limit*, but her performance in *Countess Maritza* at the Palace Theatre on July 6th 1938 was a flop.

Vera Kálmán, the beautiful showgirl who later married the composer of *Countess Maritza*, Emmerich Kálmán, remembers the reasons for the failure of the show:

"Richard and my husband were very great friends," she told me at her German retreat, set in a pine forest in Grunwald on the out-skirts of Munich, "and he begged Emmerich to have Mara in the London production of *Maritza*."

Richard was planning a world concert tour of Australia and South Africa and didn't want to leave Mara behind without work. He had a wonderful concern for his friends, and always saw that they had work, or money. Since *Maritza* had enjoyed such world-wide success, he knew it would have a long run in London, and keep Mara occupied in his absence.

"Naturally Emmerich had his doubts about Mara," Vera Kálmán continued, "for although he liked her he knew about her drinking. All the same, because of his friendship for Richard he agreed, and I remember while we were staying at the Savoy at the time of the show's run, Mara would visit us each day, apologizing for her performance the night before. It was too terrible. She had been drinking at least a bottle of cognac a day, and there was nothing we could do to stop her. This made us very unhappy because we were extremely fond of her, and she was ruining her life and the show's possible success. Unfortunately she had almost become an alcoholic and she needed more help than we could give her. She began losing work as well as her friends."

One friend who remained constant was Richard, who cast her for the lead in the South African tour of *The Land of Smiles* the following year. But once more she was continually off, and her stand-in Jose Malone had to take over the role.

After Richard's death, Mara drank more than ever. Times were bad, and Richard's widow, Diana, arranged an audition for her with the BBC. On the day of the audition, Diana took Mara home, in order to see that she got to the audition sober. She made sure that there was no liquor in the house, and went out shopping.

When she returned, she found Mara incapacitated. She had drunk some methylated spirits she had found in the kitchen cupboard.

Times got worse. Mara was out of work and friends lent her money. Then they lost contact with her and no one knew what had become of her, until Vera Kálmán heard from Mara's singing teacher in America, Emmy Kepner, that Mara had ended up in a room in Soho with a single bed, which she shared with a labourer who was working nights. He used the bed by day, and she by night. She died penniless in the nineteen-sixties, and was buried in a common grave.

Diana put an advertisement in the personal column of *The Times* asking anyone who knew what had become of Mara to contact her—but there were no replies . . .

The Singing Dream opened at the Theater an der Wien in Vienna on 31st August 1934, and featured Richard's own Tauberlied '*Du bist die Welt für mich*,' ('*You Mean the World to Me*'), which he had composed specially for Mara. A film using this title, with Rudolph Schock in the lead, was to be made years later, but it had a different story.

After a season at the Vienna State Opera as guest artiste, Richard returned to England in May 1935 to begin filming *Heart's Desire*, in which he sang the lovely *Wien, Wien nur Du Allein* ('Vienna, City of my Dreams').

But it was at the first night of another British film, *Mimi*, a dramatic film based on the opera *La Bohème*, starring Douglas Fairbanks Junior and Gertrude Lawrence, that Richard was to meet his future second wife, Diana Napier, who played Sidonie in the film.

VII
A NEW LIFE, A NEW LOVE

Diana Napier, born Molly Ellis in England in 1905, was brought up in South Africa from the age of nine. Her mother was a beautiful red-headed Irishwoman with a magnificent figure which Diana inherited; her father was a doctor of medicine who came from a Yorkshire land-owning family.

After she had been asked to leave several schools for lack of discipline, Diana was sent to finishing school in Paris, but once more her parents were asked to take her back, and in desperation arranged for her to go to Girton College in 1925, when she was eighteen. But Diana escaped through a bathroom window in search of a theatrical agent to promote her acting talents instead. She landed a role in the tour of *The Private Secretary* by Charles Hawtrey, and two years later met and married actor George Mulcaster, who was twenty years her senior. But the difference in age was too great for the impulsive, fun-loving redhead, and Diana returned home to her parents, disillusioned by marriage.

She fell in love with the well known Fleet Street artist Webster Murray, and they stayed together until her husband, who wanted to marry again, arranged to have their marriage dissolved.

Exhausting tours in plays followed. Finally, in 1927, when the Depression was creating widespread unemployment, a forlorn and dejected Diana returned home to her parents yet again.

She spent another five years on the stage, until one day she was having lunch with her godfather at the Savoy in 1932 when a tall, foreign-looking man sitting at a nearby table sent a note to her: "Are you on the stage?" "Yes I am," she scribbled back, and

Alexander Korda invited her to a screen-test for his newly formed film empire.

But Diana's relationship with Korda's London Film Productions was short-lived, due to her usual irresponsible behaviour, and her contract was cancelled.

After weeks of unemployment, the film director Paul Stein cast her for a part in his new film *Mimi*.

The rôle had its financial benefits and provided Diana with a rented home of her own in Elstree and an Austrian maid called Thea.

Diana borrowed a dress from the Spring collection of a designer friend for the film Première of *Mimi* at the old Regal in Marble Arch, and Monte Banks, who later married Gracie Fields, escorted her.

"After the show, at a party upstairs," Diana said, "Douglas Fairbanks came over to me: 'Diana, there's a man who wants to meet you rather badly. He is a famous singer, but he speaks little English.'

"I turned round and saw a fat man screwing a monocle into his right eye and beaming at me. 'His name is Richard Tauber,' Douglas continued.

"'That man!' I said, 'He was sitting a few seats away from me in the cinema. He never stopped looking at me the entire evening. I thought he was trying to pick me up.' 'He is!' Douglas laughed, 'He's simply mad about you. I'll bring him over.'

"Well, the fat man came over with outstretched hand. He took both my hands in his large fists, and I thought, 'Oh, what stiff, unattractive hands he's got!'

"'You very beautiful. I eat you, yes?' he said in his bad English. I gathered he wanted me to have supper with him. But I declined, as I was dining with Monte Banks.

"As Monte and I left," Diana continued, "I caught a glimpse of him staring after me. He looked rather sad and I felt mean for being so rude to him.

"'Who is he?' I asked Monte on our way out. 'Oh, he's a well-known philanderer,' he replied. 'Got a shocking reputation in Austria. A devil with women. I don't know how he manages. They say he's impotent.'"

Diana was to find out months later the reasons for Richard's frustrated sex life, bound up in complexes and misery from early youth. But impotent? Surely not.

A few weeks later, Diana returned from a personal-appearance tour to promote her film. As she arrived home, the telephone rang.

"You Diana Napier?" the voice with the German accent said. "Here Tauber. You play in my film. Yes? I come and see you."

She was naturally surprised at the unexpected call and the surprising offer; but before she could reply he had replaced the receiver.

"That was that Austrian singer Richard Tauber," Diana had said to her maid Thea. "Do you know him? He's on his way over."

"Know him!" cried Thea excitedly in her thick Austrian accent, "He is the greatest singer in the world, Miss Diana. And he is coming here!"

The following day, at noon, a large Daimler drove up, and Richard stepped out, followed by a chauffeur with an enormous bunch of mimosa.

Richard carried a golden cage with a pair of chirping canaries fluttering about on the bars. He marched smartly into the house, smiled broadly, and placed the cage squarely on the drawing room table. Thea practically curtsied.

"*Guten Tag, Herr Kämmersanger*," she cried adoringly.

"My language! My language!" cried Richard, kissing Thea warmly on both cheeks, then turning to a bemused Diana: "Two canaries. Easter present. One sings, the other doesn't. You no sing, Paul Stein tell me. I do. We happy, yes? You be my woman. I bring my big blue Mercedes from Vienna, yes, *schnappula*? I speak to Paul Stein; he say you play in my new film *Heart's Desire*. We write part specially for you. All settled, yes?"

But before Diana could reply, Richard discovered that there was no piano in the room. A bar, which Diana had inherited with the rented house, stood in the corner.

"A bar!" Richard exclaimed as though he had just seen the Loch Ness monster in the room. "You no drink, Diana," he insisted. "I no like women who drink!"

"No, of course I don't drink. It makes me fat. Only champagne!"

Richard turned to Thea with instructions. But he spoke German, so that Diana was only to learn later that his orders were for Thea to get rid of the bar as he was sending his piano to take its place in the corner.

Diana telephoned her agent to tell him what had been suggested about a part in the film, and later that afternoon, true to his word, Richard returned with Paul Stein, the director of the film, and Walter Mycroft, who was the head of production for Associated British Pictures. He had worked with many stars, including Conrad Veidt, Ben Lyon, Bebe Daniels and Herbert Marshall, and now Diana saw more doors opening for her too. The rôle was discussed, and arrangements made for her to start filming once the part was written in for her.

Her part was to be that of Diana Sheraton, a lady of means, who vies with Frances Wilson (Leonora Corbett) for the hero's affections. Richard played Joseph Steidler, a humble beer-garden singer in Vienna (first discovered in the film singing 'Vienna, City of My Dreams'). Frances, the sister of an English impresario, has been sent to find a tenor for a new English opera, and Steidler is persuaded to leave his beer garden for the bright lights of London under her persuasive guile for he becomes infatuated with her. But on arrival in London he meets Diana, who also falls in love with him. Disillusioned by London society, he returns to the arms of his waiting sweetheart in old Vienna . . .

One evening during filming, Richard arrived to take Diana to a cinema in Putney. He wanted her to see his film *Blossom Time*. She was enchanted by it, and fell in love with the voice and charm projected from the screen—though not yet with the actual man. As they left the pictures, Richard turned to the cinema manager and introduced Diana: "Meet my future wife, Diana Napier," he said proudly.

"Richard, you're mad!" Diana protested afterwards in the car. "I've no intention of marrying you. I don't even love you!" He smiled, patted her hand and replied, "Diana, we marry. But—first I have to tell you something very intimate. Very difficult for me to say. If—you do not understand—then we cannot marry."

She had heard more rumours about his sexual inadequacies—

about difficulties he had encountered with women; and after all, Monte Banks *had* said he was impotent. What did he want to tell her?

Yet there was something about the tubby man whose voice thrilled millions—what was it? She felt she wanted to protect this vulnerable, lovable man. His charm and sweetness, the hidden secret of his sex life made him seem a sad creature, somehow . . .

Inadequacies

Their engagement was announced in the press. The news was read on world radio, and Pathe Gazette put out newsreels. Diana was not only impressed, but regrettably overconfident at the fantastic and overwhelming reaction to their news. "Don't get a swollen head, my child," her father warned her. "Fancy wanting to marry a German Jewish singer!"

Diana felt herself falling in love with Richard. She tried to broach the subject of a normal sexual relationship: "What on earth's the matter with him?" she asked Paul Stein. "It's not natural. All he wants to do is cuddle me. He doesn't want to do anything else!"

Diana could not believe that casual petting was all he did with the beautiful and famous women he had known in his life. After all, he was a man of forty-three. Was he homosexual? she asked Paul Stein. "No. Definitely not," he replied. But he would not go into intimate details about Richard's private life.

"It annoyed me, not knowing," Diana said. "After all, I wasn't exactly inexperienced myself. I'd been married before and had had two great love affairs. My first husband was twenty years older than I was, so Richard being older was nothing new to me. Therefore I ruled out the difference in our ages as the cause.

"And then one day, he told me. We'd been out to a show, and on the way back, we stopped off for supper at the Hyde Park Hotel, where he was staying. After the meal, he sat at the piano in his suite, and played soft, dreamy music. After some time, he sat beside me on the sofa. He put his arm around me: '*Schnappula,* sweetie pie, we must talk' he said in his charming Austrian accent. 'Soon we go Switzerland and Vienna. I sing again with Mara Los-seff in my own operetta *The Singing Dream* in Vienna. You come on later. But now we talk.'"

And he began to unfold the reasons for his sexual inadequacies; his fears; and why he was afraid of a normal relationship with women.

"When I was fourteen", he began uneasily, "my father, who hadn't yet met my stepmother, had a girl friend with large breasts. While he was away, his girl friend encouraged me to lie beside her, fondling her breasts. Nothing else happened, simply that. Later in life I developed an obsession about women with large breasts—and lying beside them . . . doing nothing else.

"Before my father sent me away to study in Freiburg, he told me the facts of life. He explained that by sleeping with women I might contract a venereal disease, which might affect my brain and my voice. He said I might never sing again—and never become a great musician.

"It was a great worry to my father, but being a musician, I was more sensitive than the other boys, and I was anxious to become a singer.

"I grew up moody, and neglected my musical studies for a while—running about the town, sitting in cafés with my friends, listening enviously to them talk of their love affairs.

"This complex I developed was so strong, this fear of contracting a veneral disease, that my father's voice rang through my head every time I met a woman.

"As I grew into manhood I learned another way of satisfying my sexual desires. I learnt that by lying next to a woman and kissing her passionately I could stimulate myself, and then become satisfied. But of course this was not a happy situation for the woman, who would enjoy no satisfaction whatsoever, and that is why I have been tormented by threats of blackmail throughout my life. I did not want the world to know about my intimate private life. Every time I fell in love, I suffered the same fears. It was a nightmare, and somehow I could never forgive my father, even though I knew he did it as a form of protection.

Goethe in Franz Lehar's *Friederike* (1928).
Photograph: Ernst Schneider.

With Jarmila Novotna in Smetana's *The Bartered Bride* at the Vienna State Opera (1934).
Photograph: Dietrich-Vienna.

Arthritis attack. By ambulance to health spa (1929).

Convalescing at Pistyan Spa in Czechoslovakia (1929) prior to *The Land of Smiles* world première.

With leading lady Carlotta Vanconti (his first wife) in Franz Lehar's *Zarewitsch* (1927).

With leading lady Diana Napier in *Heart's Desire*
(they married 1936).

Leading lady Mara Losseff, *The Singing Dream*.

Canio in Leoncavallo's
Pagliacci (1936).

As Schubert in *Das Dreimäderlhaus* (*Lilac Time*) (1932).

With Evelyn Laye in the London production of Franz Lehar's *Paganini* (1937).
Photograph: George Dallison.

Recording music for the film *Heart's Desire* (1936).

Sitz Proben, conducting London Philharmonic Orchestra (1944).

Diana Napier in *Mimi* (1935).

Esther Moncrieff (1944).

Richard and Diana in Melbourne (1938).

At Anzac Memorial (1938).

"And to prove how right I was in my fear of blackmail, my first wife, Carlotta Vanconti, threatened to publish everything in the national press. How could I allow her to do it, Diana? How could I go before an audience of women again? Meet another woman without suffering humiliation?

"So I agreed to pay her large sums of money to keep her quiet. She—even made me stupidly agree to her taking a lover. I—was guilty of not consummating our marriage, and since I could not provide normal sexual intercourse with her, how could I resent her finding it in another man? So my sense of justice compelled me to give in to her demands in writing."

He paused for a moment, waiting for Diana's reaction to the disclosure and then said hesitantly: "If you can love me in spite of my—shortcomings, we can marry . . ."

The Virgin Husband

Although she came to understand the reasons for Richard's sexual frustrations after they had married, for it was indeed through her that he was cured, Diana has been interested in this question ever since. She recently asked a well-known woman gynaecologist who has a special interest in marital problems for her professional opinion on Richard's predicament.

This doctor's comments were most enlightening, and I have included them both because of the light they shed on Richard's behaviour and character, and also because they may be of more general interest: the problem is not an uncommon one, and others may perhaps benefit from knowing how it was solved in Richard's case.

About Richard's situation she said:

"The sex act is a beautiful experience designed for lovers. They use their bodies to communicate their deepest feelings. Mutual delight, physical and spiritual, may be enjoyed. Human beings are specially favoured because they can enjoy this ecstacy at any time. Other species only come together to procreate. If they enjoy it, this is of secondary significance. In human relationships the mutual pleasure should be the important thing and the child of secondary importance.

"Unfortunately, women do not know when they ovulate, so some form of contraception is always needed to prevent unwanted pregnancies. Before the days of good birth control, people were so anxious to prevent unwanted children that they did everything to make the young and fertile refrain from intercourse. Terrible calamities would happen to the boy child who played with his penis. His fingers would wither, the penis drop off, he would go crazy. The sensitive boy was terrified. Girl children were told that sex was dirty and shameful, a humiliation for the woman. Her sins would be punished by very painful childbirth and loss of respect by all decent people. Both boys and girls were warned of incurable, disgusting diseases which always accompanied the sex act.

"These frightful stories, told to children by people they loved and respected, caused great harm. When natural, good feelings of love developed, they were suppressed and distorted. Women would not allow any pleasant sensations to come from their bodies, certainly not from their sex organs. Boys were often more seriously damaged. When the penis began to erect normally, in response to early and natural sexual desire, they did all in their power to deny it. Many boys succeeded so well that they became truly impotent. Others clung to their own sex and stayed in the homosexual phase, too terrified ever to approach a woman, although they might have strong feelings towards her. Some could only approach little girls. Others clung to their mothers.

"The fear and guilt surrounding sex can only be overcome by strong true love feelings. Those who are lucky enough to meet their true love early enough, can rise above our fears and achieve the delight that we were meant to enjoy. A girl can allow the penis of the man she longs for to enter her vagina. Fear may make this painful. She may not be able to achieve an orgasm for a very long time, if her fears are strong and her love uncertain. But at least the act can be performed.

"With men, however, the penis must be erect, or intercourse cannot take place at all. It requires great desire, physical strength and determination to get the penis erect and maintain the erection

long enough to penetrate a frightened vagina. If the man's fears
are overpowering his love cannot win. The penis will not respond.
There are a great many sad couples with this problem. They can
enjoy all the love-making of the early part of the act, but they
cannot consummate their union. Many couples settle for this.
After all, it's a good form of birth control. But when a baby is
wanted they must use artificial insemination. Again, a fairly common method of achieving a baby.

"Great fears imposed on children in their early years may be
quite ineradicable. The brain can see that the fear is a myth but the
body is conditioned in its response and will not change. The only
really successful way to help a man to consummate is the love,
patience and deep understanding of a woman. When this happens
it makes the sex act a beautiful and a blessed thing indeed."

"This was the case with Richard," said Diana, who was to help
Richard to enjoy normal sexual unity.

A Continuous State of Guilt

Richard sang at an Austrian artists' charity concert at the Paris
Opèra on 27th December 1935, and was later awarded the Légion
D'Honneur for his services to charity. He returned to the Vienna
State Opera, where between January and April 1936 he sang
twenty performances of eight different operas, including another
season of *The Singing Dream* with Mara Losseff.

Diana was desperately jealous of Mara's great beauty and
couldn't understand Richard leaving Mara for her. In the years to
come, this jealousy was often to burst out anew; but it was without any real foundation, for although Mara wished to prolong her
relationship with Richard, his marriage to Diana had wholly
transformed his feelings towards Mara, so that although he continued to visit her it was now merely as an old friend who had
developed a responsible father-daughter attitude, protecting and
caring for her.

"Richard was no lover, really," Mara once told Diana in confidence, "I couldn't stand it any longer, so I drifted away from our

physical ties. But I never stopped loving him. He has always looked after me; paid my bills and helped with everything I needed. I suppose he did this out of a sense of guilt. He couldn't really make a woman happy, so he felt bound to care for her personal needs. I know that I would have starved without him looking after me.

"He was the most generous, kind-hearted man in the world. I— my trouble was that I drank too much, and Richard couldn't stand women who drank. But then I am Russian, and perhaps it is in my blood. But it got worse as I got older, and friends and theatre managements began dropping me. But not Richard. Although our love life ended in 1934, he never stopped seeing me.

"I don't know how you stood it, my dear."

"It wasn't easy," Diana had replied, "because I cured him. Doctors had told me it would take three to four years, but it only took me three months. But of course I loved him—and that was part of the cure."

Mara looked at her incredulously: "What do you mean? It was impossible to cure him. Years ago, when he was still Richard's cousin and manager, Max Tauber had gone to Vienna to see Freud, and he told him that Richard was unable to consummate any love affair, and was incapable of having children. I've known this all along."

"But I explained to Mara," Diana told me, "that after long talks with Richard I found it was not a question of his not being able to have sex at all. He was perfectly capable of having a sexual ejaculation *near* a woman, therefore he couldn't possibly be impotent.

"So I made Richard think that I was terrified of having children. That I did not enjoy sex. He then developed the ambition of being the first man who could make me enjoy sex, and in this way he forgot his complex, his nervousness and shyness. In a very short time he became a real man, and he remained capable of normal relations for the rest of his life.

"It was a terrible thing for his father to have done, to instil a young man with such fears at such an impressionable time in his adolescence.

"Once, while we were walking along the Kärtner Strasse in Vienna, looking at the shop windows, Richard saw a group of workmen. 'I am the same as them now, Diana,' he said proudly. 'Maybe we could have a baby.'

"'We could try,' I laughed. 'But what if it's born with my voice and your looks!'

"'No matter,' Richard retorted. 'I make him a singer. Tauber junior. Maybe a baritone.'

"'With *my* blood in his veins? Not a chance!'

"Although we were never to have children, Richard would often say to me with great relief, now that this great sexual anxiety had been lifted from his shoulders, 'I no longer have fears of being blackmailed. I want the whole world to know that I have a normal sex life, even though it has taken me forty-years to accomplish!'

"Little did I know then that within five years he would come to me with the news that another woman was expecting his child. . . ."

A Demanding Woman

In mid-1936 Richard and Diana returned to London from Vienna, where they had been staying at Richard's home in Schönbrunn. But their plans to marry were halted by his ex-wife, Carlotta Vanconti, who informed Richard that their divorce five years before was valid in Germany alone, and that he was still legally her husband outside Germany. She threatened yet again to take the intimate story of their married life to the press, but this time she demanded five years' back allowances as compensation.

Richard hated unpleasantness, and to avoid a scandal he paid up. But Carlotta demanded more and more money to legalize their divorce outside Germany, and, now perfectly confident of his sexual prowess, he sued her for extortion.

His father wrote to Robert Hasé, Richard's step-brother:

Dear Robert,

This attack by that Vanconti woman is terrible. Doctor Klager, our lawyer in Vienna, is here in Italy with me, and is making application to the Vienna Court of Justice for a hearing to fight her continuous demands, and to take action for blackmail. But it is not sufficient to go to Court without indisputable evidence of her blackmail in black and white, which we fortunately have, and unless attention is drawn to the witnesses which Vanconti has produced. We know who they are, and we can discredit them.

I think I have to go to Vienna early in September to be a witness on Richard's behalf and give evidence at the Court, which Doctor Klater has arranged should be heard *in camera*.

All the best,
Papa.

When Richard's father gave evidence at the hearing in Zurich he said:

"My son Richard became convinced that there was no other way of protecting himself from his divorced wife than by suing her at law.

"Carlotta extracted considerable sums from my son, who had become her springboard to fame as a singer. Not content to be the wife of a great artist, she published the assertion that Richard could only sing under her influence, and had gone so far as to tell the composer Erich Wolfgang Korngold that his voice would suffer under anyone else's training but hers.

"Richard had to bribe the director, Heinz Saltenburg, with 40,000 Rm [£2,000 in those days], to allow Carlotta to appear on the Berlin stage, for Carlotta insisted on showing Berliners how to sing Lehar, and Richard was compelled to cancel one of his own important performances in order to conduct for her.

"She borrowed valuable jewels from a leading Berlin jeweller for these performances, and when she failed to return them, Richard had to pay 32,000 Rm [£1,600] for a pearl necklace, and 45,000 Rm [£2,250] for a diamond bracelet.

"It was by no means a model marriage, and there were considerable marital difficulties in 1928. Carlotta asked for—and got—written permission to sleep with another man. She did not, however, need this permission since she had committed adultery repeatedly before this. Should he refuse to sign the agreement she threatened to go to the press with intimate details of their married life, and once he had signed it, she threatened to publish it in order to cause a public scandal unless he paid her certain sums to keep quiet.

"Richard was prepared to sacrifice a considerable amount of money in order to avoid the scandal, and in order to secure the divorce on December 8th 1928, signed an agreement under which Carlotta was to receive 150,000 Rm [£7,500] in cash certificates, paid in three instalments of 50,000 Rm [£2,500]. But six weeks after receiving the first instalment she claimed a further monthly allowance, to be paid to her for the rest of her life.

"She received the last instalment in April 1930, and shortly afterwards she made a fresh claim, for she had found that the divorce was valid in Germany alone, and should Richard reject her claim she threatened to publish a book with the title: *Liebes leben des Richard Tauber* [Richard Tauber's Love Life]. She had already found a publisher for this book, and in order to prevent publication Richard paid her a further 90,000 Rm [£4,500] with a guarantee of a further 90,000 Rm.

"After these payments she claimed more and more, so now I leave it to the judgement of the court of Justice to decide whether this is a case of extortion."

DRESDNER BANK

Depositenkasse 33
Unter den Linden 12-13
nruf: A 1 Jäger 6576, Postscheck-Konto: Nr. 1640

Berlin W 8, den ___5. Dezember 1932.

Herrn Kammersänger

Richard Tauber

Den Haag

3440

N.

WIR BUCHEN IN IHR	SOLL Reichsmark	WERT	HABEN Reichsmark
Sendung per Wertbrief an Frau Carlotta Tauber-Vanconti, Berlin	1 400.—	(Kasse)	
Sposen a/dto.	1,50		
	1 401,50	5.12.	

Hochachtungsvoll

Dresdner Bank
Depositenkasse 33

Dept. 22. 10. 32. 6000. 3.

Richard won the case, and his complete freedom from Carlotta Vanconti.

Richard and Diana were married at Marylebone Town Hall, London, on June 20th 1936. As a wedding present Richard gave Diana the rights to *The Singing Dream*, which he had composed for his ex-sweetheart Mara Losseff.

VIII
THREAT OF THUNDER

"Richard wanted to show me the Germany he loved," Diana said. "We were in Saltzburg, so we drove to Munich and had lunch at a well-known restaurant. The waiter slammed our food down on the table, and a man at the next table called, 'these bloody Jews!' Suddenly, a portly man from the next table came over to us and warned me to get Richard out of Germany at once. Naturally we left immediately, and in the car, when I asked who the stranger was, Richard replied gravely: 'Goering. Hermann Goering.' Richard then explained that Goering was a great fan of his, and had in his collection every recording he had ever made."

Months later, Richard received a letter from Goering to the effect that if he paid the £2,000 he owed in back taxes and returned to Germany, Hitler would make him an honorary Aryan. But Richard was non-political and demanded to know what his voice had to do with his Jewish father. However, he later paid the £2,000—but in order to get his father out of Germany.

Once, while singing in Coventry, he said as the bombs were falling: "Hitler has stopped me singing in Germany and Austria. He won't stop me here," and continued his performances.

"We returned to London to begin shooting Richard's new film, *Land Without Music*," Diana continued. "This was the story, based on a legend, of a small principality in the nineteenth century, whose inhabitants had taken to music as a full-time occupation, with the result that no one did a stroke of work. Pressed for payment of the national debt, the ruling princess—played by me—decided to ban all music in the principality until the debt was paid. The revolt against the decree was led by Carlini, a world-famous

tenor and native of the country—naturally, played by Richard—
who returns from abroad accompanied by a cunning American
journalist (Jimmy Durante). The rebels, armed with music instead
of weapons, win over the princess, who meanwhile has fallen in
love with Carlini, and they live happily ever after!'"

Composers' Laments

Land Without Music was directed by Walter Forde, and the music
composed by Oscar Straus (no relation to the famous Johann
Strauss) whose great success *The Waltz Dream*, first performed
in 1907, was to beat the record of Lehar's long running *The Merry
Widow*.

"In your place I would forget all dreams of great music,"
Johann Strauss had advised Oscar Straus when he was a young
man. "I would write waltzes and collect material for an operetta!
But first I would look round for a post as conductor in the provinces. There's no better place to learn your theatrical trade than
at the conductor's desk."

Straus took this advice and finally became Gustav Mahler's
assistant in Hamburg. He was later to compose the music for
Bernard Shaw's play *Arms and the Man*, adapted as *The Chocolate
Soldier*, whose hit tune, *My Hero*, rocketed him to even greater
international acclaim. But it earned not a penny piece for Bernard
Shaw, who had refused royalties from the musical and had insisted
that all scores, libretti and programmes be credited: 'Unauthorized
parody of Mr Bernard Shaw's play *Arms and the Man*.' Shaw had
not realized what success the future promised Straus and his music.

Oscar Straus wrote to Richard as follows:

Oscar Straus,   Bad-Ischl, den 27 August 1936.
Bad Ischl,
Brennerstrasse 30,
Telephon 103.
My dear Richard,

I read with interest in the magazine 'Mein Film' of your interview in which you spoke about *Land Without Music*, and your

remarks about my music made me very happy. On the other hand, I was surprised that you did not take the opportunity of mentioning my music in your statement about your concert at the Royal Opera House, Covent Garden. This would have been in the interests of both the film and me, and I am rather hurt that you neglected to include my compositions in your Covent Garden programme too. You always give only one operetta composer publicity.[1]

Some time ago, I sent you, and expressed my wish for you to sing 'Rund um Die Liebe,' ('Around Love'), and I am convinced that you would make a great success with this song that I composed specially for you.

I hear that the recording of the film has turned out very well. Unfortunately my favourite song, 'Smile for Me', has been altered, but I am sure that your musical taste has made sure that it has not been changed for the worse. I would be most grateful if you could send me the music sheet of this song with the changes, as the publishers here expect the sheet music to be exactly the same as it was when sung by you in the film.

I hope that I will have the opportunity of seeing you in London when filming is completed. It is with great pleasure that I recall the wonderful days and marvellous hospitality from you and Diana in Elstree. Please give my heartfelt regards to Diana.

With regards from Clara and myself,
Oscar.

Richard had suffered attack upon attack by composers whose works he had refused to sing. He had made a solemn promise to sing in no new operetta unless it was by Lehar, and this was to cause a rift in his friendship with Emmerich Kálmán, who had composed a new operetta for him.

Among Kálmán's successes were *Gräfin Mariza, Die Czardasfürstin, Die Bajadere, Zigeunerprimas* and *Die Zirkusprinzessin*.

The late Kálmán's Russian wife, Vera, travels the world to promote her husband's works, appearing on television and radio

[1] Meaning Lehar, of course.

shows. She dresses in Paris models and laughs about the fur coats she never finds the time to take out of store, and the jewels which cannot travel because of security and high insurance rates. She speaks in English, with an enchanting Russian accent, of her two marriages to Kálmán, of their divorce because of her love for a Frenchman and of the reconciliation and remarriage to Kálmán, thirty years her senior, when she realized her mistake.

"The rift between my husband and Richard occurred when, after the success of *Friederike* in 1928, Richard promised to sing one of Emmerich's important operettas in Vienna," she told me. "My husband was certainly delighted, and wrote an operetta called *Josephine*—with the part of Napoleon for Richard. It took him two years to complete. When he telephoned Richard to tell him he had completed the part, and asked whether he still wanted to sing it, Richard replied 'You know, Emmerich, when I give you my word, I stick to it. Just finish the work.' So my husband worked on it for a further two years, and when at last it was ready, Richard came to our house and said: 'Emmerich, I'm very sorry but I promised I would never sing any operettas except Lehar's.'

"So that was the end of any plans of working together in the future, but fortunately it did not harm their friendship."

Lehar, however, had felt that Richard was spending too much time in England and not enough on the operettas he had specially composed for him.

Rumours had spread that Lehar's publishers were about to collapse. To save himself from bankruptcy, Lehar withdrew his connections with them after the threat of legal proceedings, collected his scores, and founded his own publishing house, Glocken Verlag, which today, under the leadership of Dr Otto Blau and affiliated to the publishers Josef Weinberger, is a prominent publisher of works by many of the worlds greatest composers.

But now Lehar required the performances of his works to promote sales and launch his new company, and Richard was the greatest publicist for his music. Richard had been making films in Britain, and had not performed a single Lehar work since *Giuditta*. Lehar appealed to him to perform his works to help his publishing company find its feet. He wrote to Richard:

Franz Lehar   23rd August 1935.
Bad Ischl.

Dear Richard,

Since for me you are always the only one, I feel I can speak
openly to you. I will do everything in my power to keep us
together and I would try everything to come to London, but only
with you performing my work.

During the 1934/35 season you sang only four performances of
Giuditta at the Vienna State Opera. It seems that this was because
you found that Piccaver had learnt the role. You went up to the
office and declared that you would not sing *Giuditta* any more if
Piccaver sang your role of Ottavio. Deeply hurt, Piccaver had to
withdraw . . .

But there were other occasions when Piccaver was forced to
withdraw. Richard had guarded his roles jealously, especially
against Alfred Piccaver, in whom he saw his strongest, indeed his
only rival. He considered the English-born singer, who made his
reputation in Austria and Germany, to be the finer tenor, and felt
that he himself was considered by Piccaver to be a 'pushed-up
baritone'.

Conflict arose when, due to Richard's illness during the Drury
Lane run of *The Land of Smiles* in 1931, the impresario Stanley
Scott and Lehar, who were at their wit's end to find a replacement
for Richard, asked Piccaver to take over the rôle. But when
Richard learned that Piccaver had been approached, he went to
see Lehar.

"Franz," he said firmly, "If you let Alfred Piccaver sing my
rôle in *The Land of Smiles*, I will never, I repeat, *never* sing your
compositions again."

A distraught Lehar telephoned Piccaver and asked him not to go
to London after all, since their plans had changed.

Piccaver realized that the change was due to Richard's interven-
tion and never spoke to Lehar again.

Richard intervened once more when, during the war, Piccaver,
now returned to England, asked Richard's personal manager and

agent Eric Glass to represent him in England as well. But Richard threatened to tear up his agreement with Eric Glass if he agreed to represent Piccaver.

". . . Now comes the 1935/36 season," Lehar's letter to Richard continued. "It is now quite certain that you will not sing *Giuditta* at the Vienna State opera in this season either, which means that Vienna is closed to me. Now you want to close London for me too. The only consolation has been that you sang at the Abbazia Festival.

"Nevertheless, I want to say again that I will go with you through everything but I can't lay myself on ice. Sometimes I get the impression that you treat me as frozen meat. Believe me, what I am writing to you is no exaggeration. I hate to write all this and I am asking you to think about it and talk it over with Diana.

"My wife sends her regards. Perhaps we can find a way out of all this which will satisfy both you and me. But as you have to think about *yourself*, so I have to think about *myself* too.

All best wishes,
Yours,
Franz."

Richard agreed to sing Primus Thaller in *Kuhreigen* (*The Waltz of the Cows*) at the end of 1936, as a finale to Wilhelm Kienzl's 80th-birthday-year celebrations at the Vienna State Opera, and Kienzl wrote to him:

Bad Aussee,   16th September 1936.
Steiermark,
Austria.

Dear Herr and Friend,

I was so pleased to read in the Neues Vienna Journal of your interview in which you state your decision to sing Primus Thaller in my *Kuhreigen* at a Gast Spiel in Vienna. I can see that you had taken your solemn promise to me very seriously.

It would be advisable if you would now get in touch with the

Vienna Director so that Professor Josef Krips can prepare the work and make it impossible for them to say afterwards that they will not do the opera. It would be very valuable if you could get Novotna to sing the Blanche Fleur, a part that is excellent for her and that I have heard she would like to sing. But she has to learn it first. Will you be good enough to send her a few words on these lines?

My wife and I are looking forward to seeing you and your dear wife, and to being together with you both.

Kind regards,
Your old fan,
Doctor Wilhelm Kienzl.

P.S. I will stay here until the first days of October. Congratulations on your Legion of Honour.

There was another idea forming in Richard's mind. It was his ambition to perform an entire opera on the screen. "Why not bring to the ordinary man and woman those great classics of the operatic stage?" he asked. But the filming of an opera had always been difficult, since it demanded that the outsize performances of the large opera stages, where singers needed to project to the gods, should be scaled down to a simplified, natural style for the screen.

The German producer, Max Schach, who numbered among his previous successes *When Knights were Bold* and *Love in Exile*, and who as Head of Capitol and Trafalgar Films had made *Love from a Stranger* with Ann Harding and Basil Rathbone and *Dreaming Lips* with Elisabeth Bergner, directed by her husband Paul Czinner, chose Carl Grune to direct *Pagliacci*. Filming began at the beginning of August 1936, after Schach had agreed to pay the record figure of £18,000 for the film rights in the Leoncavallo score. But although even thirty-five years later the sound quality of the film remains supreme, it was never a financial success.

The fairy-tale atmosphere of the story was captured in the beginning with some opening sequences in colour. This was one of the first British films to use colour. The story told of the drama of Canio (played by Richard), the jealous husband, and Nedda (Steffi Duna), his unfaithful wife. Discovering Nedda's deceit, when she falls in love with Silvio (Esmond Knight), Canio stabs her during one of the performances staged by their company of strolling players. Diana Napier played Trina, the woman who discloses Nedda's infidelity.

Richard's 'On with the Motley' was one of the highlights of the film, and not only did it prove his excellent singing ability it also showed that he could act movingly under sensitive direction.

Wendy Toye, the stage and film director, arranged the ballets for *Gay Rosalinda*, which Richard conducted at the Palace Theatre in 1945. She is one of the most successful women directors in London today, and behind her are such hits as *Bless the Bride*, *Robert and Elizabeth* and the recent *The Great Waltz* at Drury Lane. She looks no different today than she did when she arranged the dances for *Pagliacci* thirty-five years ago.

"I remember one day we were rehearsing with the orchestra," she told me about the filming of *Pagliacci*, "Albert Coates was conducting, and for some reason Richard wasn't happy about the tempo. So Richard stopped the rehearsal, walked over to Albert, took the baton from his hand and said 'I show you.' And show him he did. What a difference it made! The orchestra came to life with renewed sparkle, and a hubbub of excitement swept through the studio.

"Yet he was able to do this without offending the conductor, who bowed to his fine musicianship."

After the filming of *Pagliacci* had been completed in 1936, Richard sang Mozart, Schubert and Schumann at a charity concert given at Covent Garden in September, and again at the beginning of October with the London Philharmonic Orchestra under Sir Thomas Beecham. This was followed in November with a season back at the Vienna State opera in his usual roles in *Tiefland*, *La Bohème*, *Carmen*, *The Magic Flute*, *The Bartered Bride* and *Evangelimann*. In January 1937 he created the leading role in a new opera, *Rossini in Naples*, for which Paumgartner had adapted some of the composer's music with some additional music of his own. This was followed by a tour of Egypt where, during February 1937, a special festival '*d'operas et d'operettes Viennois*' took place. Richard headed a list of brilliant artists who gave twenty-eight performances in Cairo and seven in Alexandria before they returned to Vienna for *Don Giovanni* under Professor Josef Krips.

IX
LEHAR'S DISPLEASURE

Lehar was very displeased that Richard was performing all other composers' works except his own, and during this period Richard felt obliged to arrange a London production of *Paganini*. Plans were under way for C. B. Cochran to present the show in A. P. Herbert's and Reginald Arkell's adaptation. The exquisite sets and decor were by Ernst Stern—the complete set of designs are still in existence, now the property of Raymond Mander and Joe Mitchenson, theatre collectors who are to have their own theatre museum in the new British National Theatre building.

On May 27th 1937 the curtain rose for the first time in England on *Paganini* at the Lyceum Theatre, with Evelyn Laye, who had forsaken the West End for nearly four years, and Richard, who had not been heard in operetta since the short run of *Lilac Times* in 1933. They were to take London by storm.

Paganini tells the story of the imperious Princess Anna Elisa of Lucca, said to be Napoleon's sister, a gay and passionate lady. The Princess falls victim to the spell of Paganini's music, but when he in turn is attracted by a ballet dancer, Anna Elisa orders his arrest. When he plays the violin in the Royal Banquet Hall, however, his music conquers her jealousy and when he leaves the country, she follows him to a smugglers' inn disguised as a gypsy. There they part.

Evelyn Laye and Richard had seldom been in better voice. Richard's 'Girls were made to Love and Kiss,' and 'Love, at Last,' commanded curtain after curtain, and the rapturous applause that greeted Evelyn Laye's 'Love, Live for Ever' also held up the performance. Fourteen curtain-calls and an encore at the end brought *Paganini* to a boisterous conclusion.

The evening had provided the audience with two unexpected laughs, too. One was when, during the third encore of their big duet in the second act, Richard jokingly sang some phrases into Evelyn Laye's ear—and emerged with a nose smothered in gold powder. The roars of laughter that followed were only halted by Evelyn Laye's whispering to him in between bars to remove the offending smear.

The other came at the very end when, after the curtain had risen and fallen half a dozen times, it stuck half way between the proscenium and the stage. Richard jumped up at it several times, and had to tug hard at it before it finally came down.

But box office receipts also began to fall, in spite of Queen Mary's special Gala performance. The final blow came when, even before it had reached its fortieth performance, Cochran cabled instructions to withdraw the show. Rumours circulated that the failure was due to Richard's exorbitant salary inflating production costs; but few knew that he had in fact taken an enormous cut in salary to keep the show on. Cochran, who was unable to explain the reason for its failure, published a letter in the Daily Telegraph:

"I left London [for San Francisco] in the belief that I had a success with *Paganini*. I saw the performance through on the first Saturday and the demonstration was even greater than that of the first night. On the night before I sailed, I slipped in to see the second act and there were the same encores for Tauber and Laye, and yet we never did one week's really good business. It had been said that the show was too expensive, which is entirely untrue. With the houses one expects for the first few weeks of a music show, with big stars in it, and which has had good notices, I could have had the initial production costs back in five weeks.

"Both running and production costs were less than those of Noel Coward's *Bitter Sweet* which made £50,000 at his Majesty's Theatre [which Cochran had presented with Peggy Wood in the leading role]."

Evelyn Laye

Evelyn Laye is one of the best loved and respected leading ladies of the English theatre. Star of early successes such as *The Merry Widow*, *Madame Pompadour*, *Blue Eyes*, *New Moon* and the original Broadway production of *Bitter Sweet*—and later of *Wedding in Paris*, she has only to walk on-stage at any one of the Night of a Thousand Stars Royal Gala Performances for the audience to go into raptures of applause. She is known for her stage presence and curtains—and to see her receive her audience is a lesson in the art of showmanship that only one other artiste, Marlene Dietrich, can rival.

Evelyn Laye's marriage, a romance that was the envy of the theatrical profession, ended in the death of her actor husband, Frank Lawton, not long ago. She lost not only a husband but a man who had been an adviser and stalward friend in the bleak years when the fashion for her particular kind of magic was forsaken by audiences eager for the new young generation of entertainers. But she was to become part of that same era when she played the leading lady to pop singer Mark Wynter in *Phil the Fluter* at the Palace Theatre, and scored yet another triumph.

She has large, blue eyes, beautiful fair hair, the grace and litheness of a champion greyhound, and the charm and elegance of a Vogue cover girl. She lives in an apartment in London's Baker Street, and it was from there that she told me of the recordings she made with Richard, her performance with him in *Paganini*, and their friendship.

"When I was first asked to go into *Paganini*," she recalled, "I read the script and thought 'Oh, how very old-fashioned it is,' but I thought, 'Well, there's one great reason for going into it,' and that was Richard. I was just longing to sing with him, and I was right to do so, for I learned an enormous amount from him. He was a much better musician than I could ever have become, and it was thrilling to work with him. He never, for instance, sang exactly the same twice. If we'd got a full house, all the childishness in him would rise up and he would get over-excited, and do naughty things like singing falsetto or embracing me like an ox with so much strength that I could hardly breathe. I often used to wonder whether I was going to get the next note out or not! In fact sometimes I called him an ox, to which he would reply, 'Schnappula, darling, where do you find the strength to work and sing up against an ox like me!'

"Well, I told him that I had to rest most of the day, have a jolly good steak, and then after working a couple of hours to get my voice going, I *might* have felt prepared to go on-stage with him.

"Now if I say he was temperamental, he was in some respects. I think it was caused mainly because sometimes they'd had a mis-understanding at home and you know what a misunderstanding is between husband and wife, and particularly in our business; we are inclined to over-act everything a bit. Anyway, he would come into the theatre on these occasions and pass my door—which is something he never ordinarily did. He would always knock on my door and say 'Darling schnappula, can I come in? You have some sweets for me?' And of course I had sweets for him. He was always on a diet but he liked the sweets I had for him. Only he told me never to tell Diana, who watched his diet very carefully.

"He was very generous with teaching me things; he said to me, 'I always write for you a little something at the end of a number if you want it, darling. Come bring the number to me, I will fix for you,' and he did, long after *Paganini* was finished.

"I think of him now sometimes and put on those records we made together. I know he entered into my world of musical comedy and operetta which I love today, but I'm proud I sang with him. To me, he was the king of that world."

The repeat in London of the failure that *Paganini* had already suffered in Vienna came as a blow to Lehar. He felt he had dried up; that he was unable to compose again; that Richard, the one voice for which he had composed and with which he had enjoyed such success, had forsaken him.

"I would like to compose something new," he wrote to Richard, "but I have no libretto. I received incredibly high offers from America. I accepted them immediately before, but now I want to think about them.

"I want to compose once again. *Giuditta's* première was in January 1934, and I have had no stage play since then.

"Gruder Guntram and his wife are still in Italy. I think they are preparing a new tour for next year. Could you take part?

"Please write me immediately you receiving this letter.

Yours,
Franz."

Richard's contract with director Hugo Gruder Guntram's tour arrived:

"Mr Gruder Guntram will present a Lehar Festival in the following towns under the personal direction of Franz Lehar, who will conduct his own compositions: Rome, Milan, Naples, Florence, Genoa, Trieste, San Remo, Bologna and Turin.

"Mr Tauber will sing in *Giuditta*, *The Land of Smiles* and possibly *Paganini*.

"Mr Guntram guarantees Mr Tauber forty performances.

"Mr Tauber will receive 20,000 Austrian Schillings [£5,000]. He will also receive 5,000 Austrian Schillings or the equivalent in Italian lire for expenses each day."

But this tour was not to take place until the following year, 1936, at the open air theatre in Abbazia, when Richard was to sing with Kathy Walter. This was just before the Anschluss, when so many Austrians were denied the right of continued existence in the country of their birth and as a consequence some of the greatest artistes and composers were no longer to be able to glorify their own country through music and the arts.

One such was Emmerich Kálmán, whose wife Vera puts the blame squarely on the shoulders of Franz Lehar.

Kálmán versus Lehar

Diana, Vera Kálmán and I were lunching together at Diana's home in Berkshire. It was a warm summer's day. Diana was expecting the final go-ahead by the authorities for The Richard Tauber Garden Theatre in Bracknell and Vera, who owns the rights in her late husband's music, was keen to have his works performed in the new theatre, whose function in the summer months will be primarily to perform the great operettas that Richard had sung and others composed during the period of his great successes.

Kálmán, Lehar and Richard were the closest of friends. Esther Moncrieff remembers Richard saying that if it wasn't for the fact that he was married to Lehar, he would propose to Kálmán! But when war threatened there was to be a division in the camps.

"What happened between Lehar and Kálmán" I asked Vera, "that ended their wonderful friendship?"

"It was extraordinary," she replied. "Everything was really marvellous between Lehar, Kálmán and myself.

"My husband was extremely possessive over me, and would allow me to dance with no one. His jealousy had got to the point of divorce when I left him for another man, but I remarried him when I discovered I couldn't live without him. However the only person he would allow me to dance with was Franz Lehar. Franz was a marvellous dancer, and my husband couldn't dance at all, so Frantischek used to say: 'Emmerich, let's go out dancing tonight,' and he'd kick me under the table to let me know the invitation was purely for my benefit since he knew how much I loved dancing.

"Frantischek and I would dance for a whole hour at a time and my husband would storm over to us, saying: 'Now, Frantischek, what's the matter with you? Will you not bring my wife back to me?' And Frantischek would reply with a charming smile: 'You go and pay the bill. I'm enjoying myself too much.'

"It was the most wonderful friendship. Frantischek and his wife Sophie would lunch or dine with us practically every week.

"Now when the Nazis came to us in Vienna, they wanted to know who owned our thirty-three-roomed palais. Naturally my husband said that it belonged to him, and things began to look bleak.

"As you know, my husband was Jewish. The Nazis went away, and returned a few days later to confiscate our motor cars and furniture. I was terribly frightened and realized that our money, my jewels, the house would go next. However, I went down to plead with the Nazi officers: 'Why are you doing this to us? My husband has never had political leanings. He is a gentle man. He simply composed beautiful music to glorify Vienna.'

" 'We're not interested,' the Nazi officer replied.

" 'But you yourselves are Viennese,' I said, 'You know all his tunes. They are sung daily by the nation.'

" 'Yes, yes, but he's still Jewish, and we have our orders. We have just taken over Korngold's house. That damned Jew escaped with all his money and you're not going to do the same!'

" 'My God,' said Vera, who is a Roman Catholic. " 'You've taken Korngold's house. He lives on our corner.' I felt numb. Dead inside. I knew the end for us was near. I thought what do I do? Who do I turn to for help? Who is Christian? Who is Aryan? Then I thought—there is our dear friend Frantischek! Lehar! He will help us. Certainly!

"I rushed to the telephone: 'Frantischek . . .' I could tell by his tone that he was a little nervous. 'It's Vera. Are—you all right?'

" 'How could I be all right with a Jewish wife at a time like this?' he replied. 'But you can fix things,' I reassured him, and then: 'Now Frantischek, you have been to our house. We have known you intimately for years. My husband is in trouble. I'm doing all I can for him. Please help him. He is your greatest admirer—you are his older colleague. He looks up to you. Please come over. Please put him under your protection. He's done nothing, Frantischek. He was only born Jewish. That is his only sin. Like your wife. It's not his fault. It's not hers.'

" 'Yes, yes, yes, of course,' he replied, 'But Veruschka, wait a few days, I'll see what I can do.' "

"Sophie was made an honorary Aryan," Diana interrupted.

"Yes, but later on. This was February 1938. The Anschluss began the following month, in March."

"I remember Sophie. She kept saying, 'Don't sit so close to Franz, Diana.' "

"I'm sure. She was a very jealous person. She hated my guts because Franz liked dancing with me."

" 'But you're holding his arm', she said to me. 'If you go on that way,' I replied, 'I shall hold a great deal more!'" Diana said, laughing.

"All the same, Lehar agreed to come the following day at midday. 'Tell the Nazis to come back at one o'clock,' he said, 'I will be there an hour before.' Next day eleven-thirty passed, twelve, one, two, three o'clock. No Lehar. He didn't come. He didn't show up. And the Nazis were waiting. I telephoned him at two, at three—he wasn't there.

"'Where is your protection?' the Nazi officer barked at me.

"'I—I don't know,' I said anxiously. 'Lehar is an old friend, he wouldn't let us down. He promised to come, on his honour.'

"'You must be lying. You made it up!' the Nazi shouted at me.

"*So*! I went upstairs and brought down all the Lehar photographs and letters where he had signed 'To Veruschka and Emmerich with all my love.'

"'Yes, yes, yes,' he said 'we believe you,' and they prepared to go. 'But we'll be back,' he said.

"When they had gone, I rushed back to the telephone and rang the Schikaneder Schlossel, where the Lehars were staying at the time. Sophie came on the line: 'Don't you know we have our own troubles! So don't ask Franz to come!' And she put the phone down on me.

"They let my husband down. They let him down!"

"Anyway my husband, who was Hungarian, got all the protection he needed from Horthy, the Hungarian Governor in Budapest, and we got out with everything, thank God. But the Nazis seized our beautiful home. It was turned into a hospital during the war and into Unesco Headquarters after the war. We got it back later, but we sold it. It—was a crime to sell it, but the memories . . .

"We arrived in Paris when we got out of Vienna, in time to read that Lehar had composed an overture for *The Merry Widow* specially for Hitler, who had seen it ninety times! It never had an overture before.

"There was a photograph of Hitler and Lehar, and of Goebbels kissing the hand of Lehar's Jewish wife. And my husband was finished because he was Jewish!

"Anyway, a very important man called Karl Ritter was sent to my husband in Paris by Goebbels. 'We are going to make you an Aryan, Herr Kálmán', he said, 'because one of Hitler's favourite operettas is your *Czardasfürstin*.'

"But my husband replied that he was Jewish-born, and that he would die a Jew. 'If Hitler wants me, he accepts me as I am,' he said. 'I cannot change. Besides, we are going to America in any event.'

"A little while later we read in the papers that Lehar had arrived in Paris. It was at the beginning of the war, in 1939. He came to negotiate for a theatre for his operetta *Giuditta*.

" 'I will not telephone him,' I told my husband. 'I never want to see him again!' And then someone called us to ask whether we knew that he had arrived. He had given Lehar our address in the Avenue Foch, because Lehar wanted to see us very badly.

" 'Tell him we don't want to see him again!' my husband said, and I took the telephone and asked where he was staying. At the Grand Hotel, I learned, and that he was leaving the following afternoon.

"So I went to his hotel after lunch the next day, and waited for him. An hour later a taxi pulled up outside the hotel with Lehar in it, by himself. He got out, impeccably dressed as he always was, and paid the driver.

"I went up to him. I was looking particularly beautiful that day; I was exquisitely dressed; after all, I was in Paris and it was Spring.

" 'Veruschka!' he said when he saw me, 'How wonderful! You know, I've been enquiring after you. I wanted to see you and my old friend Emmerich.'

"I looked at him steadily. I was ready for him. 'Now,' I said, 'I want to tell you that you let my husband down. It doesn't matter, your hurting me, but to hurt my husband, to let him down that way, I cannot forgive. You, whom I admired, whom I adored. . . . I'll never forgive you. 'For me, you are *dead*!'

"With that, I turned and left. We never saw him again.

"Late in 1949 we returned to Ischl and went to see his grave. My husband went inside the graveyard and called to me: 'Come, see. Sophie and Franz are buried side by side.' But I did not go in and see. Even then I could not forgive what he had done to my husband."

'You know, I'll tell you something that I've never told any-one," Diana said. "When Richard died, I had no money. I really was in a state. I had to pay for Mara Losseff's flat, and the balance of the month's rent on Esther's flat, and I had to borrow from my mother. I pawned some jewellery which I never got out.

"So I rang through to Lehar, who was staying at the Hotel Baur à Lac in Zurich and said, 'Franzel, I need a thousand pounds. I have to pay for Richard's funeral and I have no money.'

" 'I don't deal with my own finances,' he replied. 'I'll hand you over to someone else.' And with that he put the phone down, and I never heard another word from him. He did arrange a Tauber Hour Memorial radio programme in Switzerland, but it raised no money.

"Then you get a London taxi driver, who reads in that news-paper that Richard left no money, and sends me a pound." An English taxi driver, it makes you think . . .

"And when you think that Lehar had made millions out of Richard singing his songs—millions.

"But Richard was a fool when it came to money. Do you know, he sold his rights of the '*You are my Heart's Delight*' recording out-right to Odeon Records for eighty pounds. No royalties. He was on no royalties for any of his records until 1939. He only received royalties on sixty-six of the seven-hundred-odd records he made.

"The odd thing was," she went on, "that after *Giuditta*, Lehar never composed again. You see, Richard was his inspiration, and without him he couldn't compose. And when war broke out, that was the last Richard heard of Lehar. He never discussed him, and Lehar never contacted Richard until after the end of the war, in 1947, when Richard took *The Land of Smiles* to New York. The book had been rewritten as *Yours is My Heart*. But that's yet another story. Another heartbreak."

However, heartbreaks are forgotten, and harsh words heal in time. But Lehar's music will never be forgotten. He has left behind him a wealth of golden melodies, a heritage of enchant-ment and lilting strings—the magic that will live long after wars and grievances have been forgotten.

X
INTO THE STATELESS ZONE

The failure of *Paganini* upset Richard's schedule for the next few months until he was to leave for a concert tour of America in October 1937. He filled in with a seaside concert tour of England, choosing Bognor, Brighton, Folkestone, Bridlington, Scarborough and Southampton. He had chosen to sing three groups of Lieder— '*Frühlingsglaube*', '*Der Doppelgänger*' and '*Impatience*' by Schubert, '*Letzer Frühling*' and '*Ein Traum*' by Greig, and '*Traum durch die Dammerung*' and '*Heimliche Aufforderung*' by Richard Strauss.

Percy Kahn, who was to accompany him to the end of his career, played with his usual unobtrusive skill and added considerably to the success of the performances.

Richard finished the programmes with music from his films including 'All Hope is Ended' and 'Let me Awaken' from *Heart's Desire*, and 'Girls were made to Love and Kiss' and '*Fear Nothing*' from *Paganini*, to tumultuous applause.

The American tour, which was accompanied by the seventy-piece General Motors Symphony Orchestra, included guest stars Jussi Björling, Maria Jeritza and Grace Moore, who was to die tragically in a plane crash shortly before the war. The concerts began at the New York Town Hall on October 26th 1937, where Richard sang to audiences who had last heard him sing six years before. He was always met by an ovation when he stepped onto the stage. He proved once more to the American audiences his love for singing by giving wholeheartedly of himself in every performance. "His fine voice is now a little shopworn," the New York City Post reported the following day, and "the once fabulous top notes are not what they used to be. Yet it is still a remarkable regulated voice, capable of a variety of surface emotions and neatly suited to the musical exactions of Tamino's aria 'Dies Bildnis ist bezaubernd schön' from The Magic Flute, and to the coloratura demands of 'Il mio tesoro' from Don Giovanni."

This was to be followed by another concert in New York. This time Josef Schmidt was on the same bill, but regrettably he had a cold, and could not appear. Richard completed fifteen New York concerts and six radio shows before moving on to Los Angeles.

It was here, in Hollywood, that Richard's close friend Marlene Dietrich met him at the train, and presented him with a cake she had baked for him when he left; that he struck up friendships with Jeanette MacDonald, Walt Disney and Basil Rathbone and his wife Ouida; and that Diana was to catch him out for the first time and stage a jealous outburst. This last scene took place on the night of Richard's concert at Los Angeles, attended by Hollywood's greatest names, among them Clark Gable, William Powell, Edward G. Robinson and Charles Boyer, all of whom were to remain Richard's close friends.

Richard and Diana were staying at the Beverly Hills Hotel, and while dressing for the evening, Diana went into Richard's room to ask him to do up her dress. He was on the telephone, but as she entered the room, he quickly replaced the receiver.

"Who was that?" Diana asked casually.

"Oh—just a cable I sent to the promoters." Richard replied, but he wasn't a good liar; deceit wasn't in his nature. His secret telephone calls had begun to annoy Diana, and this time she was angrier than ever and decided to check up on him. She picked up the receiver and asked the operator to repeat the message in the cable Richard had sent:

It read MARA MY SWEET, EVERY HOUR BRINGS ME NEARER TO YOU. YOUR RICHARD. It was addressed to Mara Losseff in London. Diana went into a rage, and there was nothing Richard could do to stop her from leaving for New York on the next train.

"There were flowers and love letters of explanation and

apology waiting for me at my New York hotel when I arrived,"
Diana said, "but I was too upset to care.

"Richard arrived in New York the following day, after the
concert, and banged on my door to allow him to explain. But I—
just couldn't go through it all again, and I refused to open the
door."

"Diana, please!" he begged. "I have been asked to sing at the
White House tonight. President Roosevelt has asked us to dine
with him."

"But I refused to go. I've regretted missing the Roosevelts ever
since."

The Taubers returned to Europe, and at Cherbourg Richard
left the liner for Vienna. The opera season at his beloved State
Opera House was due to begin in March 1938. He sang in *The
Bartered Bride* and *Don Giovanni*. Meanwhile Diana had gone to
Switzerland on holiday, and she stayed there until February. She
went on to the South of France to stay with her mother, while
Richard began another Gruder Guntram tour of Italy and the South
of France.

He was to sing *The Land of Smiles* and *Lilac Times* in Rome,
Naples, Genoa, Turin, Florence, Bologna and Trieste, followed by
Venice, Milan, Monte Carlo and Nice. The tour began in Milan
on the 10th March, but shortly before this his throat began to give
him the usual trouble again. The manager of the tour, fearing that
this would cause a serious setback and upset the entire touring
schedule, suggested he fly to Vienna to see his throat specialist.

"Richard telephoned me from Milan," Diana said, "and told
me he was leaving for Vienna. But I warned him that storm-
troopers had massed on the Austrian border and he was not to go
for fear of his safety.

" 'My dearest Diana,' he said, 'Schuschnigg is in power. The
Nazis wouldn't dare to march into Austria.'

"So in despair I rang Randolph Churchill in London and told
him of Richard's intention to go to Vienna. 'Stop him, Diana,'
Randolph Churchill said. 'It's sheer lunacy.' I pleaded with Richard
over the telephone once again.

" 'Austria at war?' He pooh-poohed the suggestion, 'Nonsense!'

"There was only one thing for me to do. I climbed into my car and motored overnight from the South of France to Milan. I found him at the station, waiting to leave for Vienna. I managed to persuade him to put the trip off till the next day.

"The following morning he handed me the morning newspaper: 'GERMAN REICH ANNEXES AUSTRIA,' the headline read. The rape of his beloved country had begun.

"He was a shattered man. He locked himself in his room for three days without speaking to anyone, just soulfully playing the piano."

It was during this trip, when Richard was to sing at a concert in Rome for the Italian nobility, that Diana made what seemed to her at the time the *faux pas* of her life.

"Richard had gone to change, and I found myself alone. facing a galaxy of nobility in the reception room. Suddenly an extremely charming woman, whom I took to be a member of the Court, approached me and I nervously confessed my fear and ignorance of foreign Court etiquette. She smiled and assured me that she would gladly help me, and taking my arm, she steered me through a passage lined by what was probably the intimate circle of the Royal household. Now and then she would nudge me as a signal to curtsy in a particular direction, and after a few anxious minutes, the ordeal was over.

"While I was still expressing my gratitude to her, Richard returned, greeted my guide with a low bow, and presented me to her: she was Ena, ex-Queen of Spain!"

Grand Opera 'Arrival'

In April 1938 Richard returned to England, where the new Covent Garden opera season was announced. He was to sing in *The Bartered Bride*, *Die Entführung aus dem Serail*, and *The Magic Flute* for the first time at the Opera House; his English debut in grand opera, under Sir Thomas Beecham.

The Magic Flute was to be broadcast to the nation during the actual performance, and some people expressed surprise that a

musical-comedy artiste and film star should be cast for so serious a
programme; they had forgotten that before they had ever heard of
him Richard was one of the finest Mozart tenors of his day.

During the rehearsals of *The Bartered Bride* under Sir Thomas
Beecham with Richard, Hilda Konetzny and an ensemble from
Vienna friction arose between artistes and conductor. Sir Thomas
wanted one tempo, the singers wanted another. At last when the
cast were up in arms and about to walk out, Richard saved the day
by walking down to the footlights and saying to Sir Thomas:
"You must forgive us if it takes us a little longer than usual; we
have obviously been singing it wrongly for twenty years, so you
must be patient with us."

Sir Thomas was furious at first, but the air was cleared and
rehearsals continued.

Richard's reception in *The Magic Flute* at Covent Garden on
May 2nd 1938 was magnificent. Queues had formed outside in
Floral Street fifty hours before and the gallery was packed with
triumphant fans. The *Sunday Times* reported: "Richard Tauber,
as Tamino, began rather badly, but steadily improved as he
seemed to forget, and allowed us in the audience to forget, that he
was Richard Tauber and became more and more Mozart's
Tamino."

But his appearance in *Die Entführung aus dem Serail* had to be
cancelled at the last moment due to his recurring throat trouble,
and his old colleague Lotte Lehmann, who had been taken ill the
week before and had therefore been unable to sing in *Der
Rosenkavalier*, was now telephoned in the afternoon and asked to
sing the Marschallin that evening in place of Richard's programme.

Telephone calls were put through to Berlin to two other
singers, Tiana Lemnitz and Marie Luise Schilp, to return to
London immediately, to sing in *Der Rosenkavalier* that evening.

Richard recovered his voice sufficiently to sing *Seraglio* later,
and received the following notice: "It was so good a performance
that it will be a thousand pities if it is to be the only one given
during the season. Herr Tauber, though still not in the best of
voice, sang Belmonte's music with so much expressiveness and
with such a fine sense of line in the shaping of the phrases that,

With Fred Astaire in Hollywood.   *Photograph: Residenz Atelier.*

With Douglas Fairbanks Senior and Mary Pickford.

With Myrna Loy and Diana in Hollywood.

With Jeanette Macdonald.

Marlene Dietrich (1939).

Elisabeth Schwarzkopf in London (1970).   *Photograph: David Morse.*

With Grace Moore in Hollywood.

Ivor Novello in *Perchance to Dream* (1946).

Famous Korda Line-up (1936) includes: Back row, L to R: Flora Robson, Alexander Korda, Elsa Lanchester, Douglas Fairbanks Jnr., Marlene Dietrich, Richard and Diana, Tomara Desney and Elisabeth Bergner.

Front row: Conrad Veidt, Ann Harding, Victor Saville (in front), Marie Tempest, Rene Ray, Edward G. Robinson, Googie Withers.

With King Carol of Rumania.

With Maurice Chevalier during *Lilac Time*.   *Photograph: Rapid-Photo.*

besides enchanting our ears, he succeeded in giving a semblance of individuality to the character.".

And "Tauber's Belmonte was as comely a singer and as up-standing a character as his Tamino of the previous week. His tones were at all times true, but, like his acting, they seemed to lack spontaneity. There was too much of Tauber, too little of Belmonte."

For all that, Richard emerged triumphant after his coveted season at Covent Garden. After seven years in England he felt that he "had arrived in grand opera," that English opera-lovers had learned of his true worth and, for the first time, accepted him.

Down Under and Back Again

He sang a recital afterwards at Bournemouth, on May 15th 1938, before embarking for his Australian and South African concert tour. *En route* he sang in *La Bohème* at Basle on May 22nd. Then he left for Rome, from where he travelled by car to Naples, to board the S.S. *Orontes* for Australia.

A stop at Ceylon gave him the opportunity of singing on Asian soil at Colombo, where he picked up £300 for the one concert.

The Australian tour opened on June 26th 1938 in Melbourne and ended on September 29th after a total of thirty-seven concerts in Sydney, Brisbane, Adelaide, Perth, Canberra, Newcastle and Hobart.

His party included Diana, and Percy Kahn, who had accom-panied a number of the most celebrated artists of the time, among them Caruso, Melba, Tetrazzini, McCormack and Kreisler, and had also made a name for himself as a composer, his Ave Maria in particular having received world-wide acclaim.

Percy Kahn had begun his professional career as a boy soprano and had later developed as an instrumentalist as the result of a scholarship to the Royal College of Music. Apart from his musical achievements, he had a wonderful sense of humour, and was to prove the most enjoyable companion for Richard.

"The man at the piano must know every nuance of the singer,"

Percy once said, "he must practically know every note by heart, though the music is before him. He must feel the mood of the singer, recognize the almost imperceptible changes in tempo and delivery of songs and arias. In other words, there must be that secret understanding between singer and accompanist which only comes with constant practice and performance."

Australia afforded Richard a magnificent reception. Here was the star they had come to love through films and records—the man whose incomparable singing seemed to express all their own emotions and aspirations.

Melbourne completely succumbed to his charm, and his pleasure in everything he saw and did was infectious; every function he attended lost its stiffness and became cheerful and informal.

His concert at the Melbourne Town Hall was broadcast across Australia by the Australian Broadcasting Commission, which had brought him over under the aegis of Charles Mozes.

Richard's programme included Brahms, Mozart and Schubert. Brahms, referring to the composer's art, once declared that there was something to be learned from every song of Schubert. "Sometimes the secrets of Schubert are shown in a very modest way and we need, perhaps, a more pretentious composer for a guide to find them. But even with such a trifle as 'Das Rosenband'," wrote an Australian critic, "if we take an ornate setting of the words such as that of Strauss for our guide, we may see by comparison that Schubert gets in most of Strauss's points apparently without an effort, and though their expression is on a smaller scale, it is not on that account the less convincing. We find a guide, too, in such a comparison to the subtlety of Tauber's art. His programme covered a group of lieder by Schubert and Grieg, and a few popular numbers by Lehar. Not a point was missing from Grieg's 'Letzter Frühling', and comparison of its progression with the indications of the composer would have shown as perfect a fidelity to the composer's ideas as if he had been all out to sing the song for the last time in his life."

In the lighter songs, Richard was more inclined to exploit his voice for popular appeal, but despite the over-use of *mezza voce* and the occasional forcing, he lavished considerable care on the music. "After all," he said, "B flat is B flat whether it is used by Schubert or Lehar."

"Lehar feels certain qualities in my voice," he added, "and writes for me with that in mind. I love to sing his music and I think much of it will last, just as that of Johann Strauss has done. It has a genuine spontaneous gaiety."

A few days later he received a letter from Lehar:

Franz Lehar,   June 1938.
Bad Ischl.

Dear Richard,

I was deeply moved by your letter, but I find it difficult to answer. I can only say that when I hear *Paganini*, *Frasquita*, *Zarevitch*, *Friederike*, *Land of Smiles*, *Schön ist die Welt* and *Giuditta*, the music is inseparably associated with your voice. In every note I hear you. I suppose that you are now experiencing a wealth of wonderful impressions in Australia. To see the great and beautiful world has always been my dream, but I do not think that this dream will ever come true.

Did Diana tell you that I rang her up on one occasion? Unfortunately, you were not available at the time. I never received your reply, which I expected. It does not matter now, of course. On the 22nd I shall be in Nuremberg, where I shall listen to *The Merry Widow* at the Opera House.

This time I shall go to Ischl again. I shall try to create something new, but I have not yet found a suitable libretto. I have received great and unbelievably favourable offers from America. In the past I should have accepted at once, but now I am still thinking the matter over. I should like to compose again, if only just once more.

The Première of *Giuditta* took place on January 1st 1934. Since then I have written no new work for the stage. This state of affairs must change.

Novotna and Käthe (Dorsche) send their cordial regards.

I am now devoting a great deal of time to the publishing side. I have had my stage material prepared for *The Land of Smiles*, *Zarevitch*, *The Count of Luxembourg*. Now it is *Zigeunerliebe's* turn. I shall see to it that I leave absolutely first-class stage material, so that I will not be messed about with at a later date.

Gruder Guntram and his wife are still in Italy. I think they want to plan another tour for next year. Will you be able to be present then? Now do write to me at once when you get this letter.

Sophie joins me in the kindest regards to yourself and Diana.

If possible, send me some programmes,

All good wishes,
Yours ever,
Franz.

Richard's triumphant tour of Australia ended in Fremantle, where he boarded the *Anchises* for a concert tour of South Africa.

He sang eleven performances at Johannesburg, Durban, Port Elizabeth, East London and Cape Town, where he was billed as 'The Greatest Tenor in the World'. He returned to Europe on the *Warwick Castle* on November 11th 1938, with an invitation to return to South Africa the following year with a tour of *The Land of Smiles*.

A concert tour of Great Britain began on 27th November, and ended the second week in December, when he left for Switzerland for guest performances of *The Magic Flute* and *The Bartered Bride* in Zurich, Basle and Berne.

On January 14th he left Southampton for a third concert tour of North America. The grand tour progressed to Canada, with performances in Quebec, Montreal, Ottawa, Winnipeg and Vancouver, followed by Seattle.

He then moved on to California, where he took a bungalow in Los Angeles and, after concerts at Oakland and San Francisco where Hollywood stars filled the auditorium of the Hollywood Bowl, the tour raced through the East with concerts in St Louis, Boston, Detroit, Philadelphia and finally New York, from where he left America at the beginning of April 1939.

By now he had spent almost a year travelling in Australia, South Africa, Europe and America. Yet back in England he still had the vitality to sing in the provinces and on radio, and to undertake

another season of *The Bartered Bride*, this time the Czech production, at Covent Garden.

But the tiring travelling and the demands made on his voice
took their toll, and on a tour of Copenhagen in July 1939 he lost
his voice and had to cancel four concerts.

Sans Country, Sans Papers

It was now time for the promised South African tour of *The Land
of Smiles*, and Richard opened with Mara Losseff and Hella Kürty
in Cape Town on October 22nd 1939. The show was presented by
African Consolidated Theatres, and toured South Africa for ten
weeks. Richard was paid £700 a week, free of South African
taxes, together with three first-class return fares to and from the
country for himself, his wife and his accompanist, and all expenses
incurred during his stay. His leading lady, however, did not fare
so well financially. The following clause appeared in Richard's
contract:

"The Managers agree to support the Artiste with a leading lady
to be approved by the Artiste subject to her being available at a
salary not in excess of seventy pounds (£70) per week."

In other words the leading lady was to be paid ten per cent of
what Richard was to receive. Mara Losseff, however, was pleased
to appear with her old love, and the tour began.

"Although Tauber is the most brilliant personality in the show,"
one of the South African critics wrote after the first night, "he is
given full and capable support by his companion Mara Losseff as
the beautiful Lisa. She has an attractive and dominating stage
presence, and is something more than a merely competent artist
in her singing." And "Mara Losseff is a singer worthy of the
Tauber steel. She is an operatic soprano of great personal charm
and the possessor of a voice of a quality rarely heard outside the
realm of grand opera. Her production is easy and effortless, and
her voice is one of great strength and clarity."

Her drinking, alas, was to cause her to miss performances, and
her stand-in, Jose Malone, took over the role.

"Mara was such a lovely person," Jose Malone told me in London. "She had a lovely voice, and she was such a beautiful creature. You couldn't help liking her. But she liked her drink, and I was very sorry, because I had to take over the role at a minute's notice. But I didn't hold it against her—I loved her too much. Everybody did. You just couldn't help liking such a love-able, adorable person. She was shy, and seemed to cling to me. She didn't make friends easily, and Richard had asked me to stay with her as much as I could. I only went on for her a few times, but as the result of that I was asked to do a celebrity concert tour of South Africa with Richard, for which I was terribly grateful.

"It was such a pity about darling Mara—he couldn't depend on her. He never knew when she was going to keep on a top note too long—make him look silly. But she didn't do it intentionally. She wouldn't do anything to hurt or upset him. Nobody would. We all adored him too much.

"Richard should have been a terribly rich man," Jose Malone continued. "But he spent all his money on women. He never seemed to have any cash on him. He was always borrowing small amounts: 'Oh Jose, have you got fifteen shillings to lend me,' he would say, time and again.

"Women could get anything from him, but that side of him I ignored. One simply didn't take any notice of it. He was such a nice man. A charming, wonderful man. A real gentleman. One of the nicest people you could possibly work with."

Jose Malone first met Richard when she was playing the lead in Oscar Straus's *The Waltz Dream* in Belfast. The manager had told her that somebody important would be in the box that night. It turned out to be Richard, whom she hadn't yet met. He praised her voice after the performance and said he hoped they would meet again. The next time they met was at Covent Garden when they played together in *The Magic Flute* under Sir Thomas Beecham.

"I saw a lot of him during the war. He lent me his flat during the blitz. Oh, he was lovely. I had a great affection for him."

War broke out in Europe four days after Richard landed in South Africa and, being an Austrian, he found himself without a nationality, a stateless citizen, so Diana telephoned Sir George

Harvie Watt, Parliamentary Private Secretary to Winston Churchill, who was in South Africa at the time, for advice.

"Leave for neutral Switzerland and stay there until we can
arrange travel documents for you and Richard." he told her.

Fortunately the travel documents came through in time, thanks
to the efficiency of the South African Government, and Diana
received a hand-written letter from the Secretary for the Interior.

> Department of the Interior,
> Pretoria,
> South Africa,
> 13th November 1939.

Dear Mrs Tauber,

I have received your note of the 11th instant for which please
accept my thanks.

African Theatres sent my department your passport and that of
Mr Tauber last week, for the necessary visas for the territories you
are to traverse on your return to Europe by air.

We endorsed the necessary visa for Egypt and in Mr Tauber's
passport also for the British territories in Africa.

We thought it advisable to do so to obviate any possible in-
convenience to him. It was not necessary in your case in view of
your nationality by birth.

Wishing you a pleasant trip and safe return to your home.

> Yours sincerely,
> J. H. de Wet.

"We had a safe trip home, thanks to the South African Government," Diana said. "But that turned out to be the beginning of a
nightmare existence for Richard and me.

"War was to separate us. I was to fight in the Front Line, and
Richard was to fall in love with another woman . . ."

PART THREE

Troubled Times
1939–1948

XI
WAR—AND LOVE SCARS

Anxious about his passport and visa difficulties, finding himself a
stateless citizen as the result of the German invasion of his beloved
Austria, Richard, who was on his way to neutral Switzerland for
concert performances, wrote to his secretary, his step-brother
Robert Hasé, in Switzerland.

Johannesburg,
28th November 1939.

Dear Robert,

We will be returning on the same plane as this letter to you.

I'd like you to do a few very important things for me right
away. Please find out how we can extend our passports without
going to London, as I do not want to get there before March. Our
passports are only valid until February 28th. You may have to send
somebody from Switzerland to London with the passports, in
order to secure the extension. Perhaps the Home Office in London
will inform the British Embassy in Switzerland. I leave it to
you, but something has to be done immediately, as I have no
French visa, which means I could not get to London even if I
wanted to.

Please make enquiries right away. Diana would like to go to
London for Christmas, and I am in favour of it. Otherwise she
would be sitting around in Switzerland while I am singing every
night, and that would worry me.

There are definite concert booking suggestions for England, so I must know if there is any chance of getting a British passport.

Thank you for everything,
Aufwiedersehen,

Kindest regards,
Richard.

"We were glad to leave South Africa," Diana said. "The atmosphere in many parts was unpleasant, as the Boers were anti-British at the time. Bottles were thrown at Richard as he left the stage door after the last night of *The Land of Smiles*, partly as a result of his bravely striding forward to the footlights at the end of the performance when the audience refused to rise for the National Anthem: 'Have I, an Austrian, to tell you to stand up whilst we play the National Anthem of Great Britain?' he demanded.

"We landed in Rome, where we stayed for a few days to await our visas, and then we flew on to Switzerland, where Richard sang guest performances in *La Bohème* in Geneva, Zurich and Basle.

"We had decided to spend Christmas of 1939 in St Moritz, where we were to discover people of all nations—Germans, Czechs, Poles and English—who had managed to escape from Germany and Austria, staying at the Palace Hotel."

St Moritz was very gay. The attitude was 'eat, drink and be merry, for tomorrow we fight.' Diana was so incensed by the self-confident and arrogant-looking Germans 'taking over' the public lounges that she paid the orchestra twenty-five pounds to play 'We're Going to Hang up our Washing on the Siegfried Line.' She got into hot water over it, and was reported to the Embassy, but she heard nothing more about the incident.

"At last we received news that our papers were in order, the Nansen passes we had been issued with at the time of Anschluss were not valid in wartime.

"I left Switzerland a few days before Richard did, as we thought it better to travel seperately in case of enemy action.

"In March 1940 I arrived at the Dorchester, where we had taken a permanent suite.

"Just before Richard arrived in England I had luncheon with Victor Cazalet, Liaison Officer to General Wladyslaw Sikorski, then Polish Prime Minister and Commander-in-Chief of the Polish Army, and Winston Churchill. The Poles were escaping from Europe and arriving in England by the thousand to join the British Army. They included members of the 303 Polish Squadron, who were to do so much to help win the Battle of Britain.

"It was after Dunkirk and, like the British, they had been thrown into Scotland under canvas, into huts, requisitioned houses and hotels.

"'Diana,' Victor Cazalet said, 'You speak a little French and German. Would you help me with the Poles?'

"'How could I be of any help?'

"'We need ambulances. We need all the help we can get.'

"This would be more worthwhile than mooning about the Dorchester in my Hartnell models, I thought, holding the hand of the world-famous tenor whilst everyone else was doing their damnedest for the war effort. Besides, it was bound to strengthen my character. But what of my marriage, Richard's reliance on me? I knew he wouldn't like my being away. He was like a child in many ways. Alone, he felt helpless and dejected.

"All the same, I began raising money for the first ambulance. I sold some of my French and English models, asked friends for donations and finally raised enough to buy the ambulance, which was presented to General Klimenski, who was later killed with General Sikorski and Victor Cazalet in the Malta air crash over which so much controversy later arose.

"General Kliminski thanked me for the ambulance," Diana continued, "and asked who was to drive it. 'Well—er—I am,' I replied impulsively, and before I knew it, I was asked to join the Polish Army. So I went along to the F.A.N.Y. Headquarters in Victoria to join a British organization so that I could get into uniform.

"The First Aid Nursing Yeomanry had been formed in the first war, when it comprised mounted nurses, and I now found myself in the presence of a rather horsey type, who said I would have to go on a course.

"'You'll be treated like any other recruit, not like a film star,' she said, 'And no make-up.' My heart sank. However, I returned to the Dorchester, where Richard told me that I would never go through with it.

"'Yes, darling, I will. I can't sit here in a luxury hotel keeping you company now there's a war on.'"

Richard saw Diana off at the station for the course in Scotland, armed with an enormous bunch of flowers, beaming at the rest of the girls, winking at the prettiest, while Diana trailed behind like a pack donkey with two large suitcases containing her best linen and underwear, which was all to be confiscated on her arrival at the Training School and exchanged for a raw, uncomfortable battledress.

Diana returned to the Dorchester after the course with her fingernails broken as a result of working on motor engines. Her face was spotty due to the greasy food, and she looked "thoroughly awful". Richard glared at her, and then roared with laughter: "Serves you right," he howled. "You and your boom-boom ideas! Now just settle down. We have to think of earning some money."

Richard had paid thousands in back taxes on his past earnings in Britain in order to become a naturalized Briton. He had lost all the possessions and money he had left in Austria when the Germans marched in, and times were bad—even if he did continue to whoop it up at the Dorchester. He had been sending money to his father in Switzerland, and to Mara Losseff in London, and the future looked bleak.

Fortunately Harold Fielding had arranged a Spring concert tour for him, with Percy Kahn as accompanist. This was the beginning of what was to transform Harold Fielding into one of the top impresarios in Britain today.

An actor, Grenville Eves, who was stationed in Birmingham and met Richard there during the war, has one of the finest collections of Richard's recordings. He remembered a visit to one of these 1940 performances:

"Richard asked me to one of the concerts. He liked me to go round at the interval to tell him how things were going, unlike most singers who can't bear anyone near them when they work. I went round, and he asked me to bring the next morning's notices round to his hotel the moment they came out.

"The following morning I took the notices around, and he asked me to read them out. They were very complimentary, but then I came across something that caused me to hesitate: 'We felt perhaps that Mr Tauber's Lieder was not very far from *The Land of Smiles*,' it read.

"I looked at Richard anxiously, and instead of an outburst of fury he laughed, and then suddenly started singing at the top of his voice, as though I had read the most brilliant notice in the world. 'But don't you understand what it means?' I tried limply. 'What does it matter what it means?' he laughed. 'It's the way you read it that was so hilarious!'"

But when Richard returned to London after the tour, there were no more contracts. "Sweetie," he said to Diana, "how can I support you and all my girl-friends if I have no job?"

So his wife skimmed through the amusements guide of the newspaper. She jokingly stuck a pin in at random and it landed on one of George Black's shows. Although she did not know George Black personally, she telephoned to ask whether he would put on a production of Richard's *The Singing Dream*, which hadn't been performed in England before.

Cranbourn Mansions,
Cranbourn Street,
London W.C.2.
13th March 1940.

Mrs Richard Tauber,
The Dorchester Hotel,
Park Lane,
London W.1.

Dear Mrs Tauber,

Further to our conversation over the telephone yesterday, I have had a chat with my co-producer Mr Tom Arnold, who is going to ring you tomorrow (Thursday) with a view to making an appointment to go further into the suggested production.

Kind regards,
Yours sincerely,
George Black.

Helen Arnold, widow of the late impressario Tom Arnold, lives in an apartment in Baker Street. She sold her Brighton home when she found herself torn between the English South Coast and the South of France, where she owns an apartment in Cannes.

Helen's courage and devotion throughout her late husband's long illness was of an admirable constancy. She now concentrates on perpetuating his memory, and carries on the Tom Arnold tradition in a clear-sighted and well-informed way, with fresh ideas and the courage to back her instincts. It was she who had the phenomenal female impersonator Danny La Rue under contract for his remarkable new show, and offered impresarios Bernard Delfont and Emile Littler, her close friends and business associates, a share in this magnificent success at the Palace Theatre, where years before Richard enjoyed such success conducting *Gay Rosalinda*, which ran over a year.

"Tom thought Richard's *The Singing Dream* was a very good idea," said Helen Arnold. "But knowing what wartime England was like he realized it would be much too expensive and difficult to put on a new show, and suggested a revival instead.

"*The Land of Smiles* was chosen, and Josie Fearon was cast as Richard's leading lady. She had such a beautiful voice. A really heavenly voice. A rare voice, I would say," said Helen, who herself had been an opera singer before her marriage to Tom Arnold, and had enjoyed a two-year run in *Waltzes of Vienna*.

Josie Fearon, opera-singer wife of the late Gwynne Davies, who spent the last years of his life training well-known opera singers, had sung with Richard before:

"There have been three productions of *The Land of Smiles* in England," she told me, "The original one was at Drury Lane in 1931, and the next at the Dominion a year later. That was the one I first played in. Richard had never heard me sing, although I had sung several times at Covent Garden. I was asked whether I would sing for him, and when he heard my voice, I got the part.

"And then, when the revival came along, presented by Tom, I was in England with a contract to go to Zurich and South and North America, to sing in opera. There were rumours of war and I was advised to wait. I waited, war did come along of course and I was stranded in England. As I'd sung in *The Land of Smiles* before, it seemed I was the obvious choice, and I got the part. It was an extremely successful production, and ran for over a thousand performances in the course of a tour of practically the whole of the United Kingdom."

It was 1939 and Diana was preparing to leave for Scotland to join the Polish Army. "Much as I'd love to stay with you, Richard," she had said, "I'm needed. It's the least I can do for my country—the country that has given you citizenship and a new future."

"I left for military duty on May 3rd 1940, in the new ambulance," Diana recalled, "and a large Daimler that Richard had hired, packed with radios, cigarettes and chocolates for the soldiers, followed behind. Lady Bountiful was on her way to war!"

There was no equipment at the hospital where Diana was stationed, and no proper bedding. Towels and instruments were non-existent. Within a week a wounded soldier whom Diana was driving to the Scottish military hospital, died in the ambulance on the way.

"I was on my own, and unable to do anything," Diana said. "Death had really touched me, and it affected me deeply. The hospital doctor said we could have saved him, and others, if only we'd had the equipment, so I telephoned Richard with the tragic story. He realized that I was determined to stay in Scotland when I told him about the lack of equipment. 'Oh dear, schnappula, you really are taking this seriously,' he said. 'If you need the equipment, go out and buy it. Send me the bills. I'll find the money. Work is picking up and we're playing to full houses.'

"I went over with two Polish doctors and ordered the most inexpensive equipment we could find, getting really large discounts. It cost Richard over £1,500. He received a letter from the

Commander saying that when their victorious troops returned to their homeland, their President would honour Richard with the Cross of Merit; but most of them did not return to Poland because it was under Russian domination."

Richard gave away a great deal during the war, and particularly to Diana's Polish charities. He liked the Poles, who seemed to him rather Austrian in national character, and the fact that most of them spoke his mother tongue also warmed his heart. He had a remarkable memory and learned a Polish song within twenty minutes on one of his visits to the camp, and sang it without a mistake.

"But had I known that my going away would cause Richard to turn to other women in his loneliness," Diana continued, "nothing would have induced me to leave the luxury of the Dorchester, bombs and misery or not."

Richard felt dejected and became moody. He was on his own in London, far away from his German and Austrian friends. His mother had died and his father, who had escaped from Austria and gone to live in Switzerland, was ill.

In his loneliness, he turned to another woman—and confessed to Diana.

"I was stationed at the Tinto Hospital in Fifeshire when Richard arrived in a terrible state," Diana recalled. "'Oh Schnappie,' he said, 'I had an affair—it only lasted two weeks, but now, two months later, this girl rings me up. She—she says she's pregnant. What am I to do?' he said like a little boy appealing to his mother for help.

"'Why don't you let her have the baby?' I said without thinking.

"'I don't want you to be hurt,' he replied, 'Besides, I don't even love her. It—it was just one of those—those passing affairs—that went wrong . . . I wasn't careful enough. It can happen to anyone, darling, can't it?'

"When I asked whether he was sure the child was his, he replied gravely, 'It's mine all right.'

"I knew it was feasible for him to have a child, but when I realised that this affair had been with one of the sort of girls with whom he normally associated, I suggested that she might have been taking him for a ride.

"'You may be right,' he said, rather surprised that he hadn't thought of it himself. "She's probably using the child as a lever to get me to marry her! Look, I've got an idea. Write me a letter, refusing to divorce me, so that I can show it to her! Then she'll realise there's no point in going through with her plan!'

"He was so appealing and disarming, as usual, that I gave in and wrote him the letter. It must have worked, because it was the last I heard of it. But of course," Diana laughed, "It wasn't the last time he came to me with frank confessions about his girl friends. The next time he opened his heart to me, it was about Esther Moncrieff, and this time he'd fallen head over heels in love . . ."

Richard telephoned Diana often, and wrote regularly from wherever his tour of *The Land of Smiles* took him.

Grand Hotel,
Sheffield,
August 18 1940.

My beloved Schnappipie!

I am enclosing some of the notices for the tour. I am missing you very much, but I shall see you shortly when the show arrives in Scotland.

Sweety, I hope that you are not exerting yourself. Please don't diet now, you need all your nerve and energy. It is a joy that I can at least speak to you on the telephone. Work gives me a lot of peace and I hope that you find time for relaxation from work.

Otherwise each day is the same as the next. Sweetiepie, I hope to see you very soon, and that we can spend the few days we have together very happily,

Kisses, and all my love to you,
Richard.

The Queen's Hotel,
Birmingham,
August 28th 1940.

Sweety Schnappiepie,

This week has been no pleasure for me. Business was bad, and I hope things pick up in the other cities.

I am very tired here, because one cannot relax at night. Every half hour I wake and hear noises—or believe that I do. It is very nerve-racking. Otherwise I am fine.

I miss you very much, but I am glad that you are not here, under such conditions. I must keep going to the end of the tour.

I am enclosing the press cuttings. Please keep them for me.

1,000 kisses and love,
Your loving husband,
Richard.

Midland Hotel, Manchester.
7th September 1940.

Beloved Diana,

Very quickly to let you have the press cuttings and a little money. It is horrible here. I had just put the telephone down after speaking to you this morning when the sirens went. They go two or three times a night.

Do you want to get the tickets for the First Night yourself, or shall I order them from here? How many do you need?

All love and kisses, and dearest thoughts,
Richard.

By now Richard had met and fallen in love with Esther Moncrieff, and his letters to Diana showed his change in sentiment:

The Queen's Hotel,
Birmingham.
Christmas 1940.

Dearest Diana-dear!

Here I am back in Birmingham, 'celebrating' Christmas. Here, on Christmas Eve, I am singing a performance. I have never done such a thing in all my life—singing on Christmas Eve. But nowadays nothing is surprising any more and one begins to learn that nothing is impossible.

I am missing you very much, Diana, dear, and my thoughts are with you. I remember all the beautiful days of our love. Our passion for each other may have cooled down a little, but my feelings will always be full of warmth and thankfulness.

It is a pity that things had to happen this way, but one should not try to judge or condemn. On the contrary, one should make the best of it. And for that, I have the best of intentions, Diana dearest . . .

Believe me, my feelings for you will never change. It is strange that I am unable to forget everything unpleasant and painful so quickly. Only the sunny and happy hours remain.

God bless you sweetypie,
Your husband,
Richard.

First—and Second Love

At the beginning of 1941, Richard turned to his first love—conducting. He took the London Philharmonic Orchestra, founded by Sir Thomas Beecham in 1932, on tour after its first performance of the 1941 season at the Queen's Hall. The tour included Rhyl, Stratford-on-Avon, Dudley, Harrogate, Llandudno and Chester.

Although the programme varied from performance to performance, it included the overture from Weber's *Der Freischütz*, Schubert's popular Symphony No. 5 in B Flat Major, the Prelude to *Lohengrin* and Bizet's suite *L'Arlesienne*.

English concert-goers were astonished at what seemed to them to be Richard's new role, as conductor, but they flocked to the concerts, and heard him conduct his own composition, the *Sunshine Suite* of four symphonic movements, which he had been inspired to compose by his visit to South Africa.

The *Glasgow Herald*'s report on the concert described Richard's music as: "Best in the more contemplative moods represented in the first and last movements. In these his ideas are cleverly used and effectively scored. The lighter moods of the Adagio and Menuetto and the Scherzo are also clever in presentation, but not so distinctive in material. The Suite was well received." And another reviewer remarked that "This is probably the first time in history that a world-famous vocal artist has assumed such eminence as a conductor. But it is the unanimous opinion of the numerous musicians and critics who have heard Tauber's performances with the London Philharmonic Orchestra that here is one of the world's six greatest conductors. His dynamic personality and his sincere and vitalistic performances rouse his audience into the highest pitch of enthusiasm."

And Richard's father wrote:

Hotel Bristol,
Lugano,
4th February 1941.

My beloved Richard,

I hear that you had enormous success as a conductor with the world famous London Philharmonic Orchestra. I remember your childhood, when you had a dislike for your piano lessons, and you also neglected your studies at the Frankfurter Konservatory. You gave it all up without my knowledge, but resumed at Freiburg when I insisted.

You cannot deny me credit for having given you the necessary start with skills as a singer and conductor, which have now borne fruit.

As you know, I am nearly 80, and in the short time that I have to live, the feeling that I have guided and protected you during the early stages of your childhood gives me great comfort. You are living in a very sad world, and only hope and courage can help us to endure it. I have only one wish, and that is to see humanity the conqueror of all these years of misery and injustice.

I do hope that I will receive your letter in the next few days, in which I hope to read some of the things I wish to know. Our whole life here is based on 'waiting' and it would be a nice change not to wait much longer to hear from you.

To give you any advice from here would be superfluous. You

are no doubt better informed where you are. Have you composed anything new? And what are your plans regarding conducting? Perhaps you will receive some good books for a new opera.

Your loving,
Father.

XII
ESTHER

Esther Moncrieff's father, Alastair, was one of the greatest engineering inventors of his time, and became a very rich man as the result. He had supervised all the electronics on the fateful *Titanic* when he was a young man, and was later to invent the Scammel Mechanical Horse and the Karrier Cab. But he was an inveterate gambler, and towards the end of his life he lost everything he had at the tables at Monte Carlo.

He was divorced from Esther's mother, and one of his homes was in Bournemouth, where he met Richard for the first time. He was shocked to hear about his daughter's relationship with Richard, but Esther was to discover years later that he himself lived with another woman.

It was during the 1941 tour with the London Philharmonic Orchestra that Richard arrived to see Diana in Edinburgh. They went to a hotel, where Diana found him restless and preoccupied. He found it very difficult to tell her that he was deeply in love with this girl that he had met a few months before.

"He had met Esther at the Clifton Hotel in Blackpool on October 8th 1940, while he was on tour with *The Land of Smiles*," Diana remembered. "He was completely bowled over by her. She was very sweet to him indeed, extremely beautiful with dark hair, lovely long legs and a slim waist. She had the nicest nature, and Richard had completely fallen for her. But Esther didn't want him to be dishonest about their relationship, and insisted that he come into the open with me.

"Richard had an infinite capacity for love. He felt that, provided I knew he was having an affair with Esther, and she knew I knew, this would relieve his conscience. He was exceptionally open, and when he telephoned me from Glasgow, where he was playing, and said he wanted to see me the next day, on the Sunday, he stressed the importance of the meeting.

"We met at the Princess Hotel in Edinburgh, where he had taken a double room and bathroom for us to stay the night. We had a pleasant evening together, and after dinner he turned to me:

"'Sweetie pie, I have met a girl!'

"'Really, Richard, not again!' I laughed.

"'Ah, but this time it is serious,' he said. 'She is sweet, and very pretty. She is only twenty-three, young enough to be my daughter, but I have fallen in love with her. Her name is Esther Moncrieff. We met quite suddenly and I knew the moment I saw her I wanted to go to bed with her. We have a tremendous sexual attraction for one another.'

"I remember being rather shaken," Diana said. "And we went up to our room. I heard him splashing about in the bathroom, singing away. He sounded so happy, it made my heart ache. He got into bed and continued:

"'You don't mind, do you darling?' he pleaded for my reassurance. 'You see, it's because of the war. I am so lonely and I need her. I am normal with her too—the way I proved I was with you and that girl I got into trouble. You do understand, schnappie, don't you?'

"'Yes, Richard, perhaps I do. I know I can't stop you, even if I wanted to, so I'll have to understand, won't I? I hope you'll be happy with her.'"

"'When war is over, you and I will be together again, darling. I promise,' he vowed.

"And that was the end of the conversation. There was little I could do but accept the situation. After all, he was happy with her, he was sure she would do nothing to discredit him or harm his reputation, and there was no sense in my making them both feel miserable and guilty about their feelings for one another. I freely admit that I had my boy-friends, and more than my fair share too, come to that, so how could I have cast the first stone?

"We fell asleep, and the following morning he went back to Esther."

Esther Moncrieff was to devote the next eight years of her life to Richard. From the day they met she never left his side until he travelled to America in 1946 for the Broadway opening of *The Land of Smiles*, when he spent a year touring North and South America.

Esther is an attractive woman. Now in her mid fifties, she has changed little through the years. She has the same dark eyes and hair, the same slim figure, and the same ease and simplicity that appealed to Richard when she first met him thirty years before. She now lives in Brighton with her husband James, whom she married a year after Richard's death, and her attractive daughter Susan, a trained dancer, who has inherited her mother's striking good looks.

"Times aren't what they were for James," Esther told me. "He was head fashion designer for a top London dress manufacturer, but then he was made redundant after twenty-two years service, to make way for the new Carnaby Street youth craze. That was five years ago.

"Three years ago, the lease of my little boutique was taken over by the landlords, who went into liquidation a short while after, and ever since then we seem to have been dogged by bad luck."

Shortly before I went to visit her Esther had had a bad fall, when her legs got entangled with her toy poodle's lead and she sprawled headlong, breaking her left leg. She had spent weeks in hospital, and was now recovering remarkably well, but was still under doctor's orders, being visited weekly by a nurse and taking pain-killing drugs.

Her bed had been brought down to the drawing room, in the corner of which stands the boudoir grand piano that Richard had had especially made in Hamburg to fit into his cabins on world tours. Stacks of his old records stand in another corner.

From her bed she can see into her beautiful rose garden, and it was from here that she told me:

"We're really quite happy in spite of the odds. But things aren't what they were. I don't mind saying I miss my friends, all the wonderful people I met with Richard, but frankly, I just can't afford to compete on their terms. They're all so rich and successful.

"But on the other hand, we've got our daughter Susan, who is a very talented girl, and I've got memories of eight years with the most wonderful man in the world—eight years with Richard."

Esther had been going through some of the dozens of love letters Richard had written to her. Tears filled her eyes as she waded through the piles of photographs of the two of them together, or of Richard alone, many of them affectionately inscribed to her; the memories surged back. But she can never be lonely, surrounded by so much to remind her of the happy, carefree days she spent with him in shows like *The Land of Smiles, Blossom Time, Old Chelsea, Gay Rosalinda* and *The Bird Seller.*

"I met Richard through a friend of mine," she told me. "I had designed the dresses for Frances Day in *Divorce for Christabel*, which had just opened in Blackpool. I was dining with the show's producer, William Mollison, at the Clifton Hotel. Tommy Trinder and the Crazy Gang—Flanagan and Allen and Nervo and Knox—were all staying there, and they joined our party. Richard, who was also staying at the hotel while his show was in Blackpool, came over to our table and Bill said to him: 'You know all the boys, don't you?' 'Yes,' Richard said. 'But I don't know this beautiful girl sitting next to you.'

"Bill apologized, saying, 'I'm sorry, I thought you knew each other.' 'No,' Richard replied, 'but I followed the two of you along the front until you went into the Oyster Bar this morning, and I thought I would like to know her.'

"The following morning, I was having breakfast alone in the dining room. James Agate was at the next table, and Richard came down and asked to join me. The following day James Agate reported Richard Tauber breakfasting with a beautiful dark-haired girl!

"Anyway, Richard invited me to the pictures that afternoon. And that's how it all began. I suppose you could call it love at first sight. We went to a matinee and I went to see his show that night. After dinner he said it was getting late; would I like to go up and hear the midnight news with him? Next thing we were having breakfast again, and from then on, I never left his side.

"I was due to leave for Manchester the following day with *Divorce for Christabel*, but I told Bill Mollison that I had fallen in love, and he agreed to release me from the show there and then.

"I travelled wherever Richard went. But throughout those years when we were constantly moving about with his shows he still kept on our double suite at the Grosvenor House, which I must say was extravagant of him.

"He had also kept on Diana's private suite at the Dorchester until 1942, while she was up in Scotland. He just couldn't stop spending. But then he did it out of love, not out of duty."

Doppelgänger—Double Life

"I returned to my billet in Kinross," said Diana, "after Richard had told me about his relationship with Esther and had later written to me to say that he intended to bring her with him on his next visit to Edinburgh.

"Although I hadn't met her, and even though I had condoned the relationship, I couldn't face the embarrassing situation and wrote to Richard, saying so."

Kinross,
18th June 1941.

Darling,

I'm sorry, but I really cannot let you bring Esther to Edinburgh or Perth where I am so well known and respected. It would be an impossible situation for you and for me, and also very unjust to her. I know that you are being terribly talked about all over the country, but I can do nothing about it, as you have told me you can't help it. But here in this part of the world it is definitely my business and I will not be subjected to this last indignity, Richard, and I mean it. I have stood a lot of gossip for months, and sooner or later, sweetie, I am afraid you must choose between Esther and your wife. But I promised to give you till October, and I shall keep my promise.

You see, everyone, especially the Poles, think it very strange that you do not come to Kinross to see your wife, and I would hate you to give the wrong impression, because I know that you are a sweet, silly schnappie, and one day you are going to be so terribly sorry for all this.

> With my love to you always, Richard,
>   Your wife,
>   Diana.

However Richard did bring Esther to Edinburgh. He wrote to Esther from there:

> The Caledonian Hotel,
>   Edinburgh.
>   (My bedroom number is 100.
>   Sitting-room straight through
>   to no. 136!!)

Best beloved Esther!

I count the seconds till I see you again! And hold you in my arms! A car is waiting for you! If it is too late, or you are to tired, ring the porter and send the car away that has brought you this letter! I will come back to you as quickly as I can!

> love—love!
>   Of all my love!!
>   Yours,
>   Ricci.

"I was upset, naturally" Diana continued, "and turned to other men for comfort. I fell in love with a Polish officer, and when Richard returned to Scotland on tour in October 1942 with *Blossom Time*, in which Esther had a part, I asked him for a divorce to marry the Polish naval officer.

" 'Ridiculous', said Richard. 'You are my wife. How can I divorce you? Look, after the war all this will be over, and things will be the same again, huh?'

"I later discovered that he had telephoned London and arranged to have my boyfriend posted back to the Polish Merchant Navy. And that was the last I saw of him.

"Otherwise Richard behaved magnificently during the war. He continued both to send money to help the voluntary F.A.N.Y. drivers, serving under me, to buy operating equipment for the Poles and to give charity performances to raise funds.

"But he was a strange mixture of generosity and a certain meanness. He would never give his girl-friends money, for he wanted them to be dependant on him, though he paid their bills and provided everything they needed—as he did with me.

"Lea Seidl reminded me of the time when before Richard and I were married, he said I might have anything I liked at a Molyneaux dress show. I had turned to Lea and asked confidingly: 'What's the German for mink?'

"In a way I was glad of his relationship with Esther, because I knew he was making her happy as a woman. He was absolutely and completely normal with her, but as she was deeply in love with him it must have been as agonizing for her as it was for me to know that there would always be another woman on the horizon.

"Richard always wanted to have his cake and eat it too. His lack of security, this double life he led, went back to his years of doubt where women were concerned. The fear of falling between two stools kept him in love with both of us. Besides which, he was still seeing Mara Losseff."

"Diana is quite right," Esther confirmed to me. "Richard was perfectly normal with me. I used to say to him; 'Why do people go round saying you're impotent?' and he would reply, 'I was, once, but it is different with Diana and with you.'

"In some ways he was over-sexed," Esther laughed, dispelling any rumour of Richard's inadaquacy as a lover.

"The only time I hurt him," she continued, more seriously, "was when I drank. He hated me to drink. He hated *any* woman to drink. He might crack a bottle of champagne at a nightclub, or have a glass of it on a Sunday morning, but he never touched the hard stuff. His favourite drink was ginger ale and soda, although I'm sure most people who saw him drinking it would have thought it was scotch.

"I was never jealous of Richard at all, except for his piano. The thing seemed to possess him. He had to have this honky-tonk piano in his hotel room wherever he went, and when he was playing, or rehearsing with it, it seemed to exclude me from his thoughts entirely. I don't think I could have been as jealous if it was another woman. He was like a baby without it. He would sulk and not talk to anyone until we searched the town for one and had it put in his room."

Although Esther said that Diana was much nicer to her than she was to Diana, Diana told me that Esther was never unpleasant about her, and that there was no reason for her to resent her love for Richard. "We saw a lot of each other when Richard's illness began in 1947," Diana said. "Our mutual grief seemed to bring us together. I remember Richard's doctor telling me after Richard's death, that Esther had been to see him professionally, and told him that when he saw me again he was to let me know that she loved Richard very much. And I know that she did. Everybody knows it.

"Richard and I seemed to have a strange deep love for each other which surmounted all other emotions. We just couldn't be permanently parted. He demanded that I had to be at the end of a telephone and I felt the same way about him too.

"He was my anchor; my escape when any affair of mine became too serious, and the particular man with whom I was in love at the time got too involved. I always had Richard to turn to.

"I remember the time in Scotland when he really did come up trumps. I had an assignation with a rather charming English officer in a little pub in the Highlands, about forty miles from Glasgow. I arrived in civilian clothes, which was against regulations, and met my officer in the lounge. We were set to have a rather nice love affair when to my horror I saw my Commanding Officer having tea at the other end of the lounge!

"I was horrified. Trapped. I foresaw a scandal. Court-martial. The lot. So I rushed to the telephone and rang Richard in Glasgow.

Fortunately he had no matinee that day and I asked him to come over immediately. I told him I was in great trouble, but couldn't explain on the telephone.

"He didn't hesitate. He hired a car, and meanwhile I had tea with my officer under the watchful eye of my Commanding Officer, who knew me well enough to know that this man was my sweetheart, and what we were up to.

"But in bounced Richard, and seeing the officer with me and my Commanding Officer at the other end of the room, he summed up the situation in a flash. He rushed up to me, put his arms round me and kissed me, saying loudly enough for my C.O. to hear: 'Darling, I'm sorry I'm late,' and then greeted my C.O. heartily. He then turned to me and said, 'I'm sorry, darling, I won't be able to come back to see you this evening after all, so I suggest I give you a lift back to your billet now, when we're finished our tea'.

"He never reprimanded me, nor mentioned it again. But I was too frightened to go back to the pub that evening, and I never saw my charming officer again from that day to this!"

"Richard had only one fault as far as I know," said Esther with a wicked twinkle. She was loathe to mention it for fear of casting a slur on his character, but it had amused her for years, and she was longing to tell someone.

"He used to cheat at cards," she laughed. "We used to play poker, and he always used to win! Everybody *knew* he used to cheat, so he wasn't kidding anyone. But it didn't make any difference to him, he went on cheating and nobody minded. I don't know how he did it to this day, but everyone laughed about it.

"We were at the Grand in Sheffield once and a friend of his gave the most wonderful party. There was a band, and champagne till the early hours. We had a marvellous time. And then our host said, 'Let's have a game of poker,' which we did, and for once in his life Richard didn't win. He simply didn't understand how he could have lost, but he did. And our host won a great deal of money.

"The following morning, all the women received lovely, expensive presents from our triumphant host. I got a beautiful canteen of cutlery, and the men all received a Gillette razor set.

"Richard was terribly amused at this and remarked: 'He gives us a wonderful party. Music. Champagne. We play poker—he wins. The women receive expensive presents, and the men razor blades, to cut our own throats'."

XIII
UPWARD TRENDS

Richard was invited to take over the Beecham Sunday Concerts at the Albert Hall, and between September 1941 and May 1942 he conducted thirty-three times.

During this period, he had begun rehearsals for *Blossom Time*, the stage version of *Dreimäderlhause* (Lilac Time), taken from the screen version of *Blossom Time*.

After touring the provinces, *Blossom Time* opened at the Lyric Theatre in London on March 17th 1942, and record audiences flocked to this Tom Arnold production to hear Richard singing Franz Schubert's romantic story.

Anne Somerset, who was to die tragically by her own hand as the result of post-natal depression, played the dancing-master's young daughter who captures Schubert's heart. She brought an impressively youthful freshness, vivacity and gentleness to the role played by Jane Baxter in the film version.

Hella Kürty, who had appeared in the three English productions of *The Land of Smiles*, in the role she had created in Germany and repeated in South Africa with Richard, had excellent notices, as did Peter Graves, who played the Officer.

Tall, elegant, with natural charm and wit, Peter Graves is The Lord Graves in private life. He was the son of Henry Graves (the seventh Baron), and he is married to singer and actress Vanessa Lee.

"I was at Windsor, doing a play for John Counsel, and Robert Nesbitt came down and asked me if I could be released to play the Officer in *Blossom Time*," Peter told me. "And I agreed."

"The thing that I remember most about Richard when we were playing *Blossom Time*, was that we were doing two weeks at the Opera House, Blackpool, and on the middle Sunday he had promised to do a concert. He asked if I would go along and cheer him, which I naturally did.

"He was on the stage alone, wearing his blue suit, singing absolutely beautifully for almost half an hour. 'This is his métier,' I thought. I much preferred seeing him this way, without scenery or props. The costumes, and perhaps the story and the acting, somehow took away from him and his kind of charm and magic. For me he was best in his simple blue suit. Just singing."

> Hotel Bristol,
> Lugano,
> 30 November 1941.

Dearest Richard!

Robert (Hasé) has sent me the wonderful reviews you received for the tour of *Blossom Time*, and for your marvellous performance as conductor of the London Philharmonic Orchestra at the Albert Hall.

Theatre and music notices have been pushed into the background owing to reportage of war events, but even so the Swiss Press has left enough room in its papers to report on the arts abroad. The article, "Start of the American Music Season," in the midday edition, has proved how detailed the reports are, but it is very unfortunate that one seldom reads of English culture. However it said, "Richard Tauber, whose popularity in Switzerland is quite outstanding, has sent me a selection of reviews regarding his work in England, which at the same time gives one an idea about music and theatre life in England during these troubled times. He would surely be very happy if I could tell him that he has not been forgotten in Switzerland."

Meanwhile, you will have had your London Première of *Blossom Time*.

> Yours,
> Papa.

Old Chelsea

Helen Arnold told me that Richard had an idea for another show to follow the success of *Blossom Time*. This was *Old Chelsea*. Bernard Delfont presented it with Richard, Nancy Brown and Carole Lynne—who later married Delfont. It was a wonderful show, set in eighteenth-century England, that told the story of the struggles for recognition of a composer and of a pretty young milliner who helps him finally to achieve his ambition. The great hit number of the show was "My Heart and I".

The co-composer of *Old Chelsea* was Bernard Grun, author, composer and conductor. Born in Czechoslavakia at the turn of the century, Grun was educated at the Vienna and Prague Universities. He has composed music for over thirty musical plays, including *Balalaika*, *Magyar Melody*, and *Waltz without End*, and for over sixty films. He has written several books, including *The Private Lives of the Great Composers*, *The History of Operetta* and *The Prince of Vienna* (The life of Oscar Straus.)

Married to fashion designer Edith Hart, Grun has lived in London since 1935 and is regarded as an authority on the Viennese waltz. He has been musical director at theatres in Prague, Vienna, Berlin and London. He was a close friend of Franz Lehar, and his official biography of Lehar, *Gold and Silver*, published in 1970 to mark the Lehar Centenary (W. H. Allen) is a book of distinction and informed opinion.

Bernard Grun told me that when Franz Lehar introduced him to Richard, Lehar referred to Richard as "not only the *primo tenori* of our time, but also a most accomplished composer—a man with a treasure of melody in his heart."

Richard and Bernard Grun often discussed collaborating on a musical, but somehow the idea never materialized. Then one day during the war, as they walked through the glorious old-world village of Cockington in Devon, the inspiration came. It was Spring, and rhodedendrons and magnolia were in bloom. Suddenly Richard turned to Bernard and said: "Now what about this musical of ours? Isn't it time we wrote it?" "Yes, it is," Bernard replied, "but where do we take the libretto from?"

Richard suggested a Viennese setting; then a Russian; and then a Spanish; and suddenly Bernard looked round the countryside and waved his hand: "What about this? Here. England!" he exclaimed. And Richard began to call and shout: "Yes, yes, schnappula, you are right. Come on, my friend, let's begin." So they began, and that's how *Old Chelsea* was born.

Richard had written an unperformed musical years before called *Hans im Glück* (*Frank in Luck*) in collaboration with Max Hansen, and suggested using this as the basis for the new musical.

"But only two of the twenty numbers for *Old Chelsea* were taken from the old score," Bernard said, "which we rewrote anyhow. They were 'Angels Outside Heaven' and 'My Heart and I,' which even now, nearly thirty years later, is still being sung and played all over the world."

The book for *Old Chelsea* was written by the late Walter Ellis, and the lyrics by Ellis and Fred S. Tysh. The show toured Edinburgh, Birmingham, Norwich and Brighton before its opening at the New Theatre in London, and ran for a total of two years, until the middle of 1943.

Nancy Brown

Australian-born Nancy Brown began her career in England at Drury Lane in *The Land of Smiles*. Richard could hardly have known then that this chorus girl would be his leading lady in his own musical fifteen years later.

Nancy Brown has returned to Australia, and lives in Watson's Bay, New South Wales. It was from here that she recalled the two years with *Old Chelsea*.

"It was in the years of the blitz," Nancy Brown said, "and it was quite an effort to go on singing, not changing one's tempo or breathing, as the bombs dropped about us outside the theatre.

"Richard used to go in front of the curtain in a raid and say to the audience: 'You are quite at liberty to leave the theatre. There is a raid on, but I think you will be safer in here, and perhaps you will be entertained better at the same time.' I'm happy to say that no one left the theatre.

"Microphones were anathema to Richard. We got to the theatre in Sunderland one Monday morning for rehearsals, and Richard noticed three fixed microphones in the footlights. He called the manager and said: 'Mr Manager, you will remove these microphones, won't you?' and the manager replied, 'No, I'm sorry, Mr Tauber, they're fixed. They can't be moved, but I assure you they won't be on during the performance.'

" 'Those microphones must be moved!' Richard insisted. The manager, controlling his temper, retorted: 'Mr Tauber, they are *fixed*. They're secured to the stage with metal fittings and we can't move them. I *promise* you no microphones will be on.' But this did not appease Richard in the slightest.

"About half an hour before the theatre opened for the performance that night, Richard called me from my dressing room. He was chuckling the way he always did. He had a funny little laugh. He used to go: 'Tee, hee, hee, hee,' just like a naughty schoolboy. 'Come here, *Noncy*,' he said. He always called me *Noncy*. He went on to the stage in his dressing gown, poked his head through the curtain, saw there was nobody about, and with his bare hands he bent every one of those microphones flat to the boards so that they couldn't be seen behind the footlights. Of course they remained like that for the rest of the week we were there!"

Carole Lynne

Before her marriage to Bernard Delfont, Richard's other beautiful leading lady Carole Lynne, who played the milliner, had been married to film star Derek Farr.

Like Nancy Brown, Carole Lynne had graduated from the chorus. Then she was snapped up by George Black and presented as one of his starlets in *Black Velvet* at the London Hippodrome in 1939. She later made a brilliant success in *Rise Above It* at the Comedy Theatre, and was chosen by Richard for Bernard Delfont's new production.

"I was absolutely petrified when I went up for the audition for the part," the lovely Mrs Delfont told me from their beautiful

Hampstead home, "but I was fortunate to get it, and very lucky to be singing with Richard. I'd done no real big musical shows before, only intimate revues and straight shows. It was terrifying for me to sing with somebody like Richard, and I don't think I could have done it with anybody else. He was such a terrific help, and made me feel I was contributing something. I learned a tremendous lot from him; all those lovely top notes that he used to get.

"The funny thing was that I was a very young girl starting out, and he was very much older than I was, and yet I had to fall in love with him in the play. I thought, my goodness, how am I going to be able to portray this. But somehow I forgot about age. Once I was on stage with him his personality was so marvellous, he had such a sweet nature that I forgot that he was such a strange-looking man, and I really imagined myself in love with him, and I believe it came over that way."

Bernard Delfont offered Richard an exclusive contract after *Old Chelsea*, and the Delfonts and Richard remained close friends to the end.

Vanessa Lee

Vanessa Lee, who was to be one of Ivor Novello's leading ladies and close friends, understudied both *Old Chelsea* leading ladies, Nancy Brown and Carole Lynne, at the same time. Her first husband, Warde Morgan, a singer, had also appeared in the show. He was Richard's stand-in as well, and when the show opened at the Alhambra in Glasgow on November 9th 1942, Richard was off due to an attack of laryngitis, and he took over the role.

Warde Morgan had become Vanessa's Svengali-like singing teacher, and to him she owed much of the beauty of the singing that was to enchant audiences for years to come.

Vanessa's first part was in *Autumn Crocus* in 1932, she sang in BBC programmes, in *Chu Chin Chow* and *The Belle of New York*. After *Old Chelsea*, she toured with Ivor Novello's *The Dancing Years*, and went to South Africa with *Perchance to Dream*, which she played at the Palace Theatre on her return to London.

Ivor Novello wrote for her *King's Rhapsody*, in which her "Ice Princess" melted all hearts with "Some Day My Heart Will Awake", a song which she has come to make uniquely her own.

Richard and Ivor Novello were to become close friends, and often went to the pictures together, catching the matinees before their own shows. They would choose the most sentimental films and emerge with tears streaming from their eyes.

Richard had recorded "Waltz of My Heart" from *The Dancing Years* in 1936, and Novello's first letter to him was to be one of very many:

Dear Richard Tauber,

Thank you for your exquisite singing of "Waltz of My Heart" on the record. It has always been an ambition of mine to have you sing something of mine, and I'm really delighted—thank you again.

> Yours sincerely,
> Ivor Novello.

Realizing that Diana was in financial trouble after Richard's death, Novello telephoned her a week after the funeral: "Diana," he said, "I would like to organize a charity concert to raise money for you." But Diana was very proud, and declined his generous offer.

"It was a bit complicated under-studying both leading ladies in Old Chelsea," Vanessa Lee told me, laughing, "because of the fear of both leading ladies being off at the same time!"

Vanessa found one of the most endearing qualities of Richard was his sense of humour, which was almost childlike. "I remember that, when we went to Edinburgh with the show, he saw one of those large safety-pins that ladies sometimes wear on their kilts. This absolutely fascinated him. He couldn't get over it at all, so we bought him one for a present and he fell in love with it. He carried it around with him everywhere he went, and wouldn't let it out of his sight. He even took to wearing it on the stage. He'd pin it on his waistcoat, underneath his frockcoat, and when he had his back to the audience, and turned upstage to the chorus, he would open his waistcoat and show everyone this huge safety-pin."

Vanessa recalled how, when at a matinee, when the show had opened in London, and the air raids were going on hard and fast, their company was a bit short of stage staff, and the air raid warning went. The show had begun, and nobody from the audience moved. The orchestra had begun the introduction to "My Heart and I", and suddenly a huge piece of scenery started to fall, very slowly down on the cast. It was the whole side of a house. Richard had simply walked over it to, held it up with his hand, and came in dead on cue singing: "We are in love wiz you, My Heart and I—och these doodlebugs!" and of course, he brought the house down!

"He wasn't a great actor," Vanessa continued, "but his voice was absolute magic. When I first heard it, I was a child and I was fascinated by it. But the strange thing about this was that I used to hear him sing on the radio, and when I was taken to hear him sing in the theatre for the first time, I was amazed to hear the people round me saying 'Oh, but he hasn't a very big voice,' 'It isn't a very powerful voice, is it?' And this was my first reaction to artificial sound—radio, in fact, that it is so easy to turn a knob up and have volume increased—and now people have got so used to hearing this sound that we all yell and blow our heads off through a microphone. It's really rather terrifying!"

Guilt and Recrimination

Richard's relationship with Esther had deepened, but now, filled with recrimination and guilt at neglecting Diana, to whom he had not written for some months, he now wrote to her, and received her reply:

F.A.N.Y.

Kinross.

12th April 1942.

My dearest darling beloved husband,

Thank you for your sweet letter. I know all will be well between us one day—and I feel if we can brave the difficulties today our old age will hold no fears for us because we will have felt everything together; passion, loss, indifferences, jealousies and exaggerations—and we will be left with deep everlasting love and friendship. We "belong", Richard, just as your glorious voice belongs to you, and we have something secret together that only your soul and mine knows. I think our love today is greater than it has ever been.

Your devoted wife until death do us part,

Diana.

I love you.

F.A.N.Y. Headquarters,

Linlithgow,

12th May 1942.

My own darling husband,

Just a few lines to wish you a happy birthday, and to tell you once again how much you mean to me and that as long as you live I want to be your wife and your best friend. When this love for Esther is "forbei", I am here in the world, wherever we may be, for you, and *no one* can ever take your place in my heart and my thoughts.

I do not want you to ever say to me "Diana, I wish I had never married you," because I know that one day you will need me, as I need you now and always will.

Sex plays a very small part in the relationships of human beings. Especially these days when only God knows how long we shall live to see the peace of the world. How strange that I was so stupid not to understand life better when we could have been so happy. I blame only myself for everything and I know that had I been the woman I am today we would still be living in as perfect harmony as one of Chopin's musical masterpieces.

If one thinks what work is spent in composing the perfect harmony one realises how difficult it is to expect the perfect harmony in marriage; the first years of passionate ecstacy. How wise one would be if one could only use wisdom *before* the event. But out of the tangle of our marriage I really believe that our love will conquer everything and that we will hold hands together before the same home fire that we once knew through passion. I find today that sex matters so little, is so short-lived, and to quote the words of a song from *Paganini*, "life is ahead." Let us remember this on this, your birthday, and be quite quiet darling. I love you as no one in the world loves you; with understanding, with friendship and with a warm soft feeling in my heart when I think of Richard Tauber the man.

> Your loving and devoted wife,
> Diana.

> Queen's Hotel,
> Leeds,
> June 1942.

Darling Schnappula,

I am very happy that at last you have found a good billet, and at least now you have some comfort and a nice place to live in, Sweetie. I admire your war effort, and am very proud of you. Please don't overstrain yourself and look after your health.

With me everything is the same. Thank God I feel well, reasonably well in the throat which is the most important thing.

We are booked up until the 15th December (with *Old Chelsea*), then we will continue on tour wherever it is possible. I hope to God that the time will pass quickly, and I know that everything will be all right in the end.

Chin up; my love for you, Diana Sweetie, has not changed and we will go on as always. My thoughts are with you.

> With affection,
> love,
> Your husband Richard.

F.A.N.Y. Headquarters,
Linlithgow,
17th June 1942.

My own darling Husband,

Just a few lines to tell you that I shall be thinking of you on our
wedding anniversary on the 20th of June and that I do not regret
that we were married for one minute. I know that the years will
bring peace not only to us but to the world and that one day we
shall sit in the Café Bazaar in Salzburg. That you will once again
sing in your beloved Vienna Opera House, and I shall sit in my box
on the right. You will come round in the middle of *Giuditta* and
say Hullo Schnappula, then we will ask ourselves, "Was it all a bad
dream?" and answer: "No, it had to be like that to prove that real
love conquers all things, and the Happy Ending lies in our hands
whatever the future may hold." I know that we need each other
and that everything will and must be happy ever after.

Your loving and devoted wife now, today,
and always,
Diana.

July 1942.

Dearest Heart Diana,

I am enclosing a present; it is not very much, but the will to give
is there. It is a very difficult time for me, especially as I have been
without work for a few weeks. We have to economise otherwise
we can't go on, darling heart. I think I know now that you will
help me. My whole future is, if I can talk about a future at all,
dependent on that.

My thoughts are with you all the time, and soon I will be able
to see you. I think it will be possible to come for two or three days
at the end of August. I wish with all my heart that everything will
resolve itself. I believe that, and I know things will change for the
better, for our future happiness. Patience, patience. Where are the
wonderful times when I sang and you sat in the darkened box

listening? Patience, patience. I believe that I am sleeping on the top of a high precipice.

God bless you, dearest love,
From your loving husband,
Richard.

F.A.N.Y. Headquarters,
Linlithgow,
21st July 1942.

Darling Richard,

I am terribly sorry but I am starting a course on the 10th August and I simply cannot get off it as it is an Army order, so if you come to Scotland on the 9th I can only spend one evening with you, and I must leave without fail at 7.30 in the morning. So I really feel, Sweet, that it would be better for you not to come at all just now, and perhaps we could arrange a visit later in September when I shall have a long leave and could come see you in London. I do not know what to say or to suggest. Of course if you could catch the last train on Saturday evening—the 10.55, we could have all Sunday together as well as the evening.

I have never worked so hard in my life and I am very tired of it all and wish this bloody war was over and we could get back to our life again.

All my love darling. I love you so much and miss you more and more every day.

Your loving wife,
Always and always,
Diana.

Conflict

Richard wrote to Diana that the tour of *Old Chelsea* in which Esther Moncrieff had a part was to visit Scotland. But Edinburgh, where the show was to open, was Diana's base, and Diana foresaw an embarrassing situation. She wrote imploring him not to bring Esther to Edinburgh, where she was known and respected as the famous tenor's wife, but Richard wrote back explaining that Esther was in the show, and that he could hardly "send her away like a servant".

He nevertheless managed to change the tour date to Glasgow instead, however friends would still have expected Diana to visit her husband in Glasgow.

Diana wrote angry letters of protest. Richard replied in German, in which he was better able to express his feelings:

> Midland Hotel,
> Manchester,
> 24th October 1942.

Dearest Diana Heart,

The tension between us at the moment makes me very unhappy since there should be no differences between us at this particular time. I have thought of finding a just solution for a long time, and have come to the conclusion that it is impossible for me to accept your wish and your suggestion in respect of your visit to Glasgow. I can understand the situation in Edinburgh where you are stationed, and I respect your position there in the army.

I shall do everything in my power to avoid your meeting Esther in Edinburgh under the present circumstances, but in Glasgow it is different.

You must understand that it is impossible, no matter how you feel about her, impossible for me to send her away because she is so dear to me and I value her very much.

The change in the bookings from Edinburgh to Glasgow will make it much easier for you to explain your not being able to be with me, as you will be on a course in London. After your return from London, may I suggest you and your Army friends come and see the show. Afterwards, I can come with you to Linlithgow, or meet you in Edinburgh.

I have three matinees in Glasgow, so I will be in the theatre most of the time. I will come over to meet you in Edinburgh on Sunday the 15th and we could have a lovely day together. Perhaps we could drive somewhere in the country. This is only a suggestion. The decision rests with you.

But I would like to point out that it would be wise to think about the matter as it would save us sorrow and unpleasantness. One should really not make life more difficult than it already is, and don't forget that we have to expect a lot of worthwhile things for our future.

Dearest heart, I have not written a letter like this to you for years. I have opened my heart to you, and appeal to you. Now it's up to you. A discussion may help us to evaluate the situation and find out what is in each other's heart.

Please read this letter very carefully. Ask someone to help you with the translation, but I have to write in German to express my inner feelings, and it would be terrible if you were to misunderstand them. My love for you makes it possible for me to write this letter. My love is based on friendship and understanding, and it will never change.

I greet you, and embrace you with all my heart, as long as you want me to love you.

> Your loving husband,
> Richard.

Papa Tauber

Richard's father died of cancer in a Swiss sanatorium in 1942. War had left him a stateless citizen, unable to settle anywhere. Money was short, and Richard, who had transferred £150 a month to him through the Bank of England, was to hear from him for the last time.

> Sanatorium, Lugano,
> Switzerland.
> 24th May 1942.

My beloved Richard,

We have been very close to each other, and I must therefore now write to you—for what may be the last time. The allowances you sent me through certain channels do not compensate me for the bitterness of my life at present, which will continue to the end, the terrible situation I have been placed in due to lack of money, going from one country to another, not being able to stay anywhere without citizenship permits. I know you are trying to get money to me through the Bank of England, but the fact that the Swiss banks freeze the money does not help my bitterness.

It is a calamity that I should find myself in such a financial situation at my time of life.

I will spare you the details of my unfortunate position, but this I feel is my last performance, lying here in bed writing to you, and therefore my writing is bad. I have one last wish, and that is to be cremated where your stepmother and my other friends rest.

I am sending you a ring I have worn all my life through Swiss friends who are leaving for England shortly. Keep this as a remembrance of me. Perhaps it will bind us together in the next life.

Be proud of your voice, and of England.

My thoughts will be with you on all your ways hereafter.

God bless you and I hope the Allies win the war.

I have suffered a lot over the war, but now I suffer from actual physical pain.

> I embrace you,
> Your
> Papa.

President Franklin D. Roosevelt.

(*Left*) Beniamino Gigli (1931).

(*Opposite top left*) *The Evangelist*'s composer Dr. Wilhelm Kienzl (1933).

(*Opposite top right*) Composer Eric Wolfgang Korngolz (1921).

(*Opposite*) Gigli, Chaliapine and Richard in London.

(*Left*) Lawrence Tibbett (1939).

Franz Lehar and Richard as Prince Sou-Chong in *The Land of Smiles* (1929).

With composers Emmerich Kalman and Franz Lehar.

Franz Lehar.

In New York (1946). Framed: Franz Lehar, Esther Moncrieff, Charles Boyer, Edward G. Robinson. Group: Clark Gable, Diana, Myrna Loy and Richard.

Richard Tauber. One of the greatest lyric tenors of the age.

Diana and Richard leaving Guy's Hospital after operation for removal of his lung. The last photograph taken (1947).

Photograph: *Associated Newspapers Ltd.*

XIV
LETTERS OF LOVE ANEW

Richard spent the next two years, between 1942 and 1944, conducting the London Philharmonic Orchestra on tours throughout Britain.

Diana was now stationed in London, where she was office bound. She was never really to forgive him, for his association with Esther had become public knowledge and he was living openly with her in his double suite at Grosvenor House while Diana stayed down the road at the Dorchester.

"We had a tiny kitchen in our suite at the Grosvenor," Esther said. "We had bought one of those small Belling cookers, because Richard adored eating at home.

" 'Oh schnappie,' he would say, 'please don't let's go out tonight, darling. Make one of your gorgeous goulashes.'

"I had a wonderful woman, who used to work for Diana before Diana went up to Scotland. She used to come occasionally when we weren't very late. She would also help me with my washing and ironing. It was difficult to find anyone those days, and even more difficult to provide meals of goulash in wartime England with our supplies of coupons!

" 'My darling, my dearest schnappie,' Richard would say with childlike excitement, rubbing his hands together as he sat down, 'we're eating at home tonight. Isn't that marvellous!' And he would tuck into the goulash like a child with a giant bowl of ice-cream.

"He would derive such pleasure from the simplest things in life."

Diana decided to go overseas in order to save face. This had the effect of making Richard return to her periodically before she left. He loved the secrecy of creeping round to her suite at the Dorchester, dining out with her, and then running back to the Grosvenor House not breathing a word of it to Esther.

Late in 1944 Diana managed to get herself posted to the Polish Red Cross in Belgium with the help of General Maczek, the Commander in Charge of the First Polish Armoured Division. On her arrival in Belgium she became the only British woman in the fighting division in Polish history; this was prior to the Warsaw uprising, when many Polish women became fighting soldiers. She was to be the only English woman to win the Cross of Merit, the highest Polish award.

In London the blitz showed no signs of letting up. However this did not deter Tom Arnold and Bernard Delfont from mounting a revival of *Die Fledermaus*. Their English version of the Richard Strauss operetta was called *Gay Rosalinda*, and Richard was asked to conduct. He had been suffering from throat trouble, and the invitation gave him an opportunity to rest his voice.

Gay Rosalinda

Irene Ambrus, one of the stars of *Gay Rosalinda*, was instrumental in persuading Tom Arnold and Bernard Delfont to present the show.

She told me that Eric Charell, who discovered her at the age of seventeen, was also responsible for her becoming a star in Berlin. Her uncle was the director of one of the theatres in Budapest, and when he heard her sing after dinner at home one day, he said: "This girl has got a wonderful voice."

"Then why don't you give me a part in one of your shows?" she asked jokingly—and he did! In Berlin Charell heard about her success in this show, and offered her a part in a large Berlin production, but she didn't want to leave Budapest. However she did go in the end, and thereafter appeared in several Berlin productions. She came to England in 1934.

She had made a success on the continent in *Die Fledermaus*, and she asked Bernard Delfont if he wanted to put it on in London.

"Jack Hylton sent a telegram to Max Reinhardt—whose version it was," she said, "saying that he would produce it, but not with me in the part. He wanted someone else—someone he was rather keen on at the time. Anyhow, Reinhardt cabled back saying that he knew me and considered me right for the part.

"I worked twenty-four hours a day trying to get the show on—raising the money, finding backers—but everyone said it was too strenuous an operetta to run continuously, that it couldn't run more than a week. Well, after the year-long run, they ate their words!"

It opened at the Palace Theatre on February 25th 1945. It starred Ruth Naylor, Irene Ambrus and Cyril Richard. Esther Moncrieff played Molly, Irene Ambrus's sister. Peter Graves played the leading rôle of Count Orlofsky.

"Of course, the great thing about it," Peter Graves said "was that nobody really looked at us up on the stage at all. They had all come to see Richard conducting! I mean, we were all acting our heads off and cavorting away, but he was being marvellous down in the orchestra pit, and stole the limelight.

"His great habit was to sing along with us. He had, after all, played my part in Berlin and Vienna when he was young, and knew it backwards."

Peter had a song right after his entrance in the second act. It was rather a good entrance, and Richard used to vary it when he came on. Sometimes he would let Peter come on with no music, and then to amuse himself and Peter, and because he loved practical jokes, he would instruct the orchestra to play more or less anything they fancied in order to make Peter laugh, and add more sparkle to the scene.

"The song was called '*Chaqu' un à son goût*'," Peter recalled, "and one night, when the show had been running for nine months, I gave him the cue for the music—and nothing happened. No music. So I looked down, and there he was, slumped in the conductor's chair. Sound asleep. He'd dropped off. So I got up, went down to the footlights, said my line again, loud and clear at him, and he sprang up, raised his baton, and the music played!

"But of course he'd got the giggles and so had I. I had no breath left to sing and neither of us could continue. It brought the place down, and for the first time we had an ovation for that number!"

Conductor Eric Robinson had worked with Richard during the BBC radio shows and put the orchestra in at the Palace Theatre for *Gay Rosalinda*. "I must say," Eric said, "that it was amazing to find how not only did the orchestra enjoy everything he did in the way of conducting, but every night there would be a little queue of star artistes and chorus by the pass door. When he conducted the overture they would sneak out and just stand there in the darkened aisle to watch him conduct. He created this fascination for them every single performance."

Discussing Richard with Eric Robinson was Felix Aprahamian, the music critic. "Well, you know, Eric," he broke in, "he had exactly the same fascination for the musicians in the London Philharmonic Orchestra." (Mr Aprahamian was a member of that orchestra at that time.) "In fact, when he wanted to work with a concert orchestra, he would give his *Gay Rosalinda* company a fortnight's tour with you.' And of course the orchestra adored him. The performances were absolutely fabulous. They regarded his interpretations of some of the big classic like Beethoven's Pastoral Symphony, for instance, on the same level as the performances of, say, Beecham and Erich Kleiber, with whom they had worked. They had immense respect for him as a musician and a conductor."

"Well I certainly had a great respect for him as a singer when I accompanied him so many times," replied Eric, "and I shall always think what a pity it was that we didn't get more recordings out of his conducting."

"But had he realized, say, in the mid-forties that his singing years were limited and had he set about learning a bigger repertory, he might with good health, have had, another quarter of a century of conducting life before him."

"But to ask Richard not to sing," replied Eric, "would have been asking a bit too much."

"Yes, but how good a conductor was lost in him," said Aprahamian.

"Yet we must forgive him, you know."

Your loving husband, Richard

Despite his success at the Palace, Richard was to miss Diana more than he had anticipated and, once again filled with remorse and recrimination, for he and Esther were well settled by now, he wrote to Diana abroad again and again. But his letters were often delayed, as she was in the front line, and when he went for months without a word from her he became anxious.

Grosvenor House,
19th January 1945.

Dearest Heart Diana,

My love will follow you wherever you go. My thoughts will always be with you and my belief in our future will give me the strength to survive our separation and all it's longing.

Let me congratulate you on your courage and willpower to do this great work. The reward will come by itself.

Grosvenor House,
February 1945.

Darling Heart,

Last night I got your letter—thank you. It was only the second letter I got from you, but I am very sad that you have not received my long one, I wrote a few days after you left. I gave it personally to Captain Hockman who saw you in Brussels and rang me up a few days ago. I gave another letter to Captain Walsh when I visited him at the Polish Club. I also gave a letter to Mr Budding and went to see him at the Polish Embassy.

Grosvenor House,
March 1945.

Dearest Diana,

I have not been able to ring you or cable you and this is the worst for me. Not even to know where you are, where you live, or how you live. O sweety love, it will be a good lesson for me—and when you are back, everything will be cleared up and settled.

I can't write very much what I feel and so I think because my lonely heart just misses you, there is no way of expressing it. Be good, my love. Take care of yourself, and relax as much as you can.

My thoughts will be with you always and protect you wherever you are.

I kiss you with all my love, longing to hear from you, and hoping that you may be back in April.

Grosvenor House,
April 1945.

Sweetie Pie,

I just received two nice letters from you at the same time. One dated the 25th and one the 28th. I am just going to the theatre for the matinee, but I wanted to get this off to you today.

Don't worry, everything will be as you see it in your nice letter. I dream of it, and see us on all our nice plans, we will be again together.

Don't worry, dearest, about Esther. Well, I have to go some-where to eat after the show, so therefore I go with her or Alexa.[1] That is the only time I am really with Esther. But I try to be with other people, so we hardly see each other, and I think in time she will live her own life. I arrange it like that as much as I can, because you know I love you and everything will be all right.

14th May 1945.

My beloved Sweetheart,

I still have no letter from you since 16 days. Why my sweet? I miss you very much. You are such a brave schnappie, and I want to say that I am very proud of you. The time will come when we will be together, and we'll remember all the years of hardship and separation, and all will seem like a dream.

Please darling, whatever happens, please keep thoughts of me, it will be worth it in the end, and will not be in vain. I know that my future is only with you, and my life will prove it to you.

[1] His secretary, Alexa Weir.

Don't forget your husband who loves you forever,
P.S. I am so worried about the war and not hearing from you.

19th May 1945.
Dearest Diana,

Oh, why don't I hear anything from you? My birthday, the 16th, without a single line from you. I have just now a lot of nasty troubles and no message from you, and it doesn't make me feel any better. It's impossible for me to write to you all the things that are happening here, but there is one thing that I can tell you—there is still the possibility of our going to America.

His subsequent letters reveal his anxiety both over his throat trouble and at not hearing from Diana.

9th June 1945.
Dearest Diana Heart,

Now I am really very upset. I got the three letters from you in one week saying that you didn't get my letters. I don't know what to say any more. This is the fourth letter in the last nine days and I am very sorry and sad about it. My love and thoughts are always with you, my dearest, but there are days when I am more depressed and my throat is not very good at the moment. I have a lot of worries and I don't know how I get on, but I will get over it.

Through my cancellations, I lost a lot of income.

5th July 1945.
Dearest Heart,

Received your letter from 29th today and am very sad and upset. Yes, I am upset that you did not get all my letters I wrote you the last three weeks and more. Above all the letter about our Anniversary day [June 20th].

My throat is not well yet. I had to cancel three weeks' arranged broadcasts and several Tuesday concerts.

Darling, I am in an awful mess at the moment and everything is upside down. I hope all will go well and we see it through.

I have to fight through. I have to fight it alone, and I will.

I promise you—because I know that you are the only one in my life. Please believe me. All else is nothing. All love and thoughts.

Diana had finally written that she hoped to be demobbed, and expected to arrive in London in October. But the hotels were full and finding a room for her was difficult. When she did not arrive as expected, he wrote to her:

> Grosvenor House,
> 22nd October 1945.

Dearest love,

As arranged, I rang Saturday night and Sunday morning. Unhappily you didn't arrive! I rang again this morning, but no schnappula. You said you would send me a cable, if you were not going to Antwerp. In any case I was very disappointed because I looked forward to speaking to you again. You wrote to me that you would not go to Belgium on your way back here.

Please write more nice letters. I miss you very much dearest. My film will be completed in two weeks, and I begin my broadcast series again every Sunday 7.15–7.45 beginning on the 4th November.

The broadcasts continue till we leave for America. This time the broadcasts go out "live."

> Your loving husband,
> Richard.

The film Richard referred to in this letter was British National's *Waltz Time*, directed by Paul Stein, with Anne Ziegler, Webster Booth, Carol Raye, Patricia Medina, Peter Graves and George Robey in the cast.

The story concerns the young Empress Maria of Austria, who falls in love with a captain in the Imperial Guard. He refuses to marry her because of the unnatural conditions imposed by her counsellors. They part, but in true musical comedy style are reconciled, and succeed in introducing the waltz to the Court, where it has hitherto been forbidden.

This was to be Richard's penultimate film; the last was *The Lisbon Story*, in which he sang "Pedro the Fisherman".

Ronnie Waldman, who was the producer of the BBC's *The Richard Tauber Half-Hour* radio show, is now Managing Director of Visnews, which is affiliated to BBC Television.

"In the world of entertainment and the arts," he told me, "it is not uncommon to encounter people who have two entirely opposing strands in their personalities. This was certainly true of Richard. On the one side he had this extraordinary, almost child-like enjoyment of life, and on the other side there was the hard, tough, shrewd perfectionist, entirely professional in his work.

"This gave me great delight because I was producer of all the radio programmes he did in the series in 1945, 1946 and 1947. It was a great time and Richard did some superb performances in those programmes with great guest artistes like Lionel Tertis, Leon Goosens, Moura Limpany and so on. Of course, Richard was singing the entire range of music that he was so good at.

"When we started, the programme went out on the Allied Expeditionary Forces programme, and the orchestra was all in uniform. It was conducted by Regimental Sergeant Major George Melachrino and the leader of the orchestra was Sergeant Eric Robinson. But the moment V.E. Day came, that band, which had been known as the British Band of the A.E.F., was transformed into the Melachrino Orchestra, and the shows went on and on.

"Richard enjoyed the programmes, but I'm sure he found them hard work. On the other hand, his enjoyment of hard work was part of his professionalism, and his tough professionalism was demonstrated by one extraordinary incident."

It was Christmas 1945. Richard's programme was going out on the air on December 23rd. Ronnie Waldman wanted something a little different, and instead of booking the usual type of guest artiste he chose the Luton Girls Choir. Richard had never heard of them, and when Ronnie said they were amateurs he was furious.

He wasn't going to have amateurs on his programme. In vain Ronnie protested that they made the most beautiful sound of this kind that he had ever heard; "No amateurs!" Richard insisted.

"Look, Richard," Ronnie had said, "we've had arguments before, and we've managed to settle them amicably. You trusted me before—trust me now. Wait until you hear them at rehearsal." He was taking a big chance.

The rehearsals were in the BBC's huge Maida Vale studio and Ronnie called the girls half an hour before Richard was due to arrive. They were singing Landon Ronald's 'O Lovely Night', when the door burst open at the far end of the studio, and Richard came in. And stopped—and stood transfixed.

"It seemed to have the most extraordinary effect on him, the sound of these pure girls' voices," Ronnie said. "He stood absolutely still, and didn't move a muscle until the end of the song. And then, very slowly, he walked across the full length of the studio towards the girls, and as he got towards them, I saw tears pouring from his eyes . . .

"He held his arms out to them, unable to say a word. From that moment on he was their slave. It was Richard who did so much to make them the success they became."

XV
DOWNWARD SLOPES

After the year-long run of *Gay Rosalinda*, Richard went to Zurich to see Franz Lehar to discuss plans for a Broadway production of *The Land of Smiles*. From there he wrote to Esther:

> Hotel Baur au Lac
> Zurich
> Wednesday 22nd May 1946.

Dearest Heart,

Oh love! It is wonderful here is spite of today's bad weather. The air is wonderful. I am having a fine time here seeing all my old friends and sitting with them, talking about old times! Nothing and nobody has changed here! One has the feeling that time has stood still!! Ah yes, my love, I miss you—I have such an eager longing for your presence that I am quite severely and often depressed. *Now* I can reach you over the telephone—quite easily—but how will it be when I am far away? I will not think of it!

Write a note to me. All love and dearest thoughts.

> Yours ever,
> Ricci.

War was now over, and Diana returned to England in August 1946.

Richard left for New York for rehearsals for the American première of *The Land of Smiles*; Diana was to join him there later.

Filled with enthusiasm, he was optimistic about the Broadway opening, and wrote to Esther, telling her so:

Hotel Pierre,
New York.
7.30 a.m.
Monday August 12th 1946.

My beloved heart,

Everything is wonderful and great and overpowering here. There is nothing you can't get. The tempo pushes you along. And then you suddenly feel alone and homesick for your little England with all its faults and misery. And you can't help feeling sorry for this meek little lamb you left behind with all its dearest memories!

Alexa[1] arrives soon, for I must have someone with whom I can talk and do my little things, and build a bridge between you and me and my thoughts and feelings.

Enjoy yourself and be a good girl!

God bless you—you know where I am always. Cable or write to me. This will be my dearest pleasure and recreation here. It will give me strength and endurance, till I have you back.

8.45 a.m.

Dearest,

I got your letter this very moment. Tears came into my eyes. And I have to read it twice, because I could not read it properly! My sweetest love! Every word was so dear and heart-warming— touched me to the core! Please write more, my love. It will be the food for my soul. Thank you my love. Today, Monday, we start rehearsals all week, and I think it will be all right. I have not seen the girl who plays *MI* yet! The theatre is very nice but the dressing room in very small.

I love you with all my thoughts,
Ricci

By now Diana had arrived in New York. She would see Richard in their hotel suite, writing to Esther. He would look over his shoulder at her, and with the smile of a naughty boy say: "I

[1] His secretary, Alexa Weir.

should have been a sailor, not a singer, with a girl in every port!"

"Letters would come from Esther," Diana said, "and he would sometimes read extracts to me. 'Esther is in Paris.' 'Esther is back in London.'

"To me, this was his greatness. His honesty. I felt it was far better than the usual lies and inevitable scandals and divorce which so many people go through. Richard was never two-faced, yet he always felt insecure. I think he wanted to be sure that as he grew older he would never fall between two stools and end up without me or Esther. Selfish—yes, I agree—but that was Richard.

"I could never condemn him for his human qualities and human weaknesses, for he lived for his music. This took first place, and everything else, including his loves, came next.

"Richard wanted to be the same great lover in life as he portrayed in his great love songs. With him it had to be: 'To understand is to forgive.'

"I felt one of the most important aspects of his character was his attitude to the women in his life.

"Once one looked after him in a wifely way, and tended to his needs, he developed a motherly love, as he did in my case; or a father-daughter relationship would develop, as in Mara Losseff's case, and eventually in Esther's case too. The moment this feeling ruled his emotions, sex went out of the window.

"Had I remained the spoilt little film star, Richard would probably never have looked at another woman.

"But now, in New York, he was alone at the helm—and before him lay one of the roughest seas of his career."

The book of *The Land of Smiles* had been revised to suit American tastes, the cast had doubled, and the scene had been moved to Paris. It was retitled *Yours is my Heart*, and Richard was only to discover the disastrous changes at the start of rehearsals, by which time it was too late to effect any improvements. He found comfort in writing to Esther. She had had hopes of making the trip to New York as well but did not want to reach any decision until the show opened and showed signs of success. However, she went to the South of France on holiday, and Richard, unable to contact her on the telephone, wrote:

Hotel Pierre,
New York
22nd August 1946.

Dearest Heart Esther!

My love! You know I must be very brave, because it tempts me so often to pick up the telephone and try to reach you! But I know it is hard and unpleasant for both of us. And oh, at the end, when one finally gets through and can't hear a word! So I have to leave it alone, but I miss you very much. It is only to hear your beloved voice! I hope you're enjoying your holiday. I think of you every moment I can spare. I have not had the courage to stay home by myself during the evenings. I can't bear it. I just can't bear it. So I go out, and come home more tired, and fall into bed, incapable of thinking. Yes, my love, I miss you.

So don't forget me—send me a short cable. A few words only. They will give me such stimulation. I will try to ring you in Paris! Send me your Paris hotel address.

Now, God bless you, my love,
I kiss your dear eyes,
And when I close my eyes,
I feel the touch of your slim fingers on my cheek—

Ricci

And on his opening day:

Hotel Pierre
New York
Thursday 5th September 1946.

Dearest Heart!

The great day is here. And when you get this letter, it will all be over!

The cable you sent gave me a wonderful feeling and I'm taking it with me on stage tonight! *Thanks*!! I am going to the theatre in two hours, and while you sleep, I shall fight one of the greatest battles of my career.

God Bless you my own love,

I have to move Monday to the Stanhope Hotel, 5th Avenue. All love and thoughts.

Your fare to New York to join me will be with you tonight when I look into the audience,

Yours ever,
Ricci.

Yours is my Heart opened at the Schubert Theatre that evening, September 5th 1946, with an all-American cast. Ethel Merman was playing *Annie Get Your Gun* at the Imperial Theatre, *Oklahoma* was playing at the St James Theatre and *Carousel* at the Majestic. Ray Bolger was at the Broadhurst Theatre, and Basil Rathbone in *Obsession* at the Plymouth. Richard's 'pantomime' didn't stand a chance, the cynics said.

"Unhappily, the musical called *Yours is my Heart* is uncomfortably dull and most clumsily staged," a critic wrote. "I kept wishing, towards the middle of the second of the three acts, that the stage manager would send the company home and let Tauber come down front and give us a repertory of those fine German and Austrian romantic songs, starting off with *Wien, Wien* . . ."

Although the critics panned the show, the audiences flocked to hear Richard. But he developed further throat trouble, and was unable to go on. His stand-in John Hendrick took over the part, and although he gave a fine performance, Richard's absence became the talk of New York and audiences dwindled.

Richard saw one specialist after another, but there was no improvement, and the show faced financial disaster. Then he seemed to rally, and his reappearance was advertised. Audiences flocked once more, but when the night came he was unable to go on after all and Diana found herself before the curtain making a speech of apology for his inability to appear.

New York,
Monday 30th September 1946.

Dearest Heart Esther!

Well, I have the mood! These are the most depressing and miserable days I have ever had. I am starting again tomorrow,

Tuesday, trying to save what there is to save. If it is not possible, well, we've had it—

Love, everything is so different from what I had expected! I wish I had stayed home with you instead. Oh darling, I am so homesick, oh so homesick. Maybe I'll be back early (at least to Europe) much earlier than I expected.

Oh Schnappipie! I love you—and I can't be without you. Please wait for me!! Maybe you will go into a show until I come back—or till we know *exactly* what is going to happen *here*! Everything is so uncertain. So mixed up. But one thing is sure. I am coming back to you as soon as I can. I think I will live in Park West as well!! I can have all my things in 811 and live with you in 627. I dream of it already now!

> All love and kisses,
> Your Ricci.

Things went from bad to worse. The producers had decided to take the show off, but Richard managed to find another backer and it was given a two-week reprieve. But it was to no avail. The failure of *Yours is my Heart* proved a disastrous shock for Richard, who was now stranded in New York. He had been there a considerable time without earning a penny, and this stop in his income left his finances in a more precarious position than ever. He wrote Esther, trying to explain.

> The Stanhope,
> New York.
> Friday 4th October 1946.

Dearest Heart!

Well darling, the last 12 days were the darkest of my life. You will never know what I went through here. When you get this letter, perhaps all is finished and decided already. The enclosed newspaper cutting will show you the situation. If we close, then I have of course a few offers for concerts and radio, but that is not really what I want. But what can I do? I have to do it for a few weeks to get along. I am sure I will be in Europe by the end of the year. I

can't go back to England at once but I can go to Switzerland and
wait there till everything is arranged in England (tax-wise!)

Oh love, if you only know! The days are long and endless. I
haven't been out of my room for ten days except to see the doctors
—and the nights often follow with sighs and tears. Yes, darling. I
am not ashamed to say it.

God bless you, my only one—think of me and wait for me and
the good old times. They *must come back* and they *will come back*.
They say there is sunshine after rain—and I could use a few sun-
rays!

My thoughts are with you,

Ever,

Your Ricci.

Yet his financial position did not curb his telephone mania, and
his bills rose to astronomical heights. He was an inveterate telephone talker. His telephone bill in America for the season amoun-
ted to over 3,500 dollars. His arthritic wrists had rendered him
incapable of shaving himself, and he had gone through life calling
on the services of barbers to shave him wherever he went. He once
telephoned from New York to let his barber at the Dorchester
know when he would be arriving in London. From London he
had telephoned Diana from the War Office—a quite unprecedented, not to say unheard-of, thing to do—to the front line, to
let her know that he'd sent her some Marienbad tablets in case
she'd had constipation!

"He would telephone me from New York to my flat in London," Esther told me, "and talk till the early hours of the morning.
I used to say 'What on earth are you doing, calling me this time of
the night?' 'It's cheaper!' he would say, and go on and on talking!"

The Stanhope
New York
15th October 1946.

Esther love! Dearest Heart!

Just to tell you that you made me very happy with your sweet
telephone call last night, which was the first real good thing I have

had all the last unhappy weeks. *Thank you my love*! I never felt your nearness to me so much before. I had fallen asleep a few minutes before and then I heard your soft voice in my ear—as though you were in the room with me. Oh love! There will still be a few months for me to roam so we must suffer separation. Perhaps it is a good thing, for it will clear away all misunderstandings and show us both that we cannot live without each other.

I do love you—and always will,

Your

Ricci

New York, 18th October 1946.

Dearest Heart!!

Just a few words to tell you that I love you, and that I am dreaming every day in this most unhappy period of my life; dreaming of the days in future when we can be happy again, and share together all those dear things—I miss more than anything!

When I can lay close to you and tell you the story of these dark days—and feeling home again . . .

Please wait for me my darling—these months will pass—and at the end of these long months of waiting and longing, a very happy future. . .!!

I have to pull through here. I have to keep alive and working hard—but I could not do so without your help.

Your own,

Ricci

New York, 26th October 1946.

Dearest Esther Heart!

Just a few lines to tell you that I feel better and that I've become a human being again. Yesterday I started singing and rehearsing for the tour. All goes well again; the voice is fresh and clear as usual.

I am now definitely starting my first concert on the 12th November in Ottowa, then the 14th, Montreal, and then one other on the way back to New York. I will be back here on Sunday 17th. The dates after this are not fixed definitely but I will let you know everything, my love!!

Ah Love, where are you now? I do miss you.

At the moment I can't afford anything—not even to send Diana back. I have been, and am still in an awful mess!!

I have no money on me and the Bank is closed so I shall send you some with the next letter. If you want to write me a letter, do so *soon*, as I may get it (*must* get it) before I leave on the 9th or 10th!

Be a good girlie and don't forget that there is a Heart far away from you and always near and close!!! By the way, I mean *my* heart!!!

Ricci

The Stanhope
New York
27th October 1946.

My dearest Heart!

I do love you.

I do miss you so much. I know that everything will turn out alright, my dearest!

Patience, my love!

A few months only!!

I have to pull myself together and make what I can here, whatever I do.

I *must* make up for my bad luck. For you and me!!

I must have the foundation of *our* future happiness!

Think of me often—often my Esther, love, for I shall think of you always.

Ricci.

A concert at Carnegie Hall was organized, and Richard sang Giordano, Méhul, Schubert, Grieg and Léhar to a packed audience. George Schick, his musical director for *Yours is my Heart*, accompanied him at the piano.

Schick who was born in Czechoslovakia and had made his debut as conductor at the Prague Opera House in 1927. He conducted Sir Thomas Beecham's Czech production of *The Bartered Bride* at Covent Garden in 1939, and went to America the same year as musical director to Risé Stevens, the American mezzo-soprano.

Moved by his recovery, Richard's lifelong friend Marlene Dietrich, who was at the Carnegie Hall concert, met him backstage with tears of joy in her eyes.

Alexa Weir, who had been Richard's secretary for the past eight years, left Carnegie Hall with Richard after the performance. A young man dashed up to Richard in the street, exclaiming eagerly: "May I shake your hand, sir. My father knew you. He said you were one of the finest tenors he had known, and one day I would hear you. I thought your performance tonight was . . ." "And who is your father?" Richard interrupted, "He was Enrico Caruso, sir." "Then it is *I* who should shake your hand." Richard replied.

He visited Canada with his recital, but returned to New York dejected and disillusioned with his financial position. He was finding it virtually impossible to make ends meet, and wrote to Esther:

> The Stanhope,
> New York
> 18th November 1946.

My dearest Esther heart,

I am back from Canada! Very nice and very successful but very tiring and cold!! The flight back was wonderful. Now I am back again—and "out of work" til the evening of December 2nd. Oh, lovey, it is very hard work going on like this and I am very depressed that everything has gone so wrong. I was "myself" a bit in Canada because of the sunny and nice people, and the work—and money! But back here in New York I again feel the depressing outcome of this unfortunate affair!! But I have to pull myself together and not let it get me down.

Oh dearest heart, why didn't I stay home? Oh dearest—why? I am always very glad when I have a little talk with you, but

often during the day I get sad and homesick and often want to
throw the whole thing up and just go home—but with what?

Tell me dearest—write to me—what are you doing? Are you
going to our little Places—the Savoy—Grosvenor—and our
beloved Cinemas? I often dream of it all.

Love and kisses, my beloved darling,
Your Ricci.

Diana returned to London, for money was shorter than ever
and an economy of some sort was essential. She left on the *Queen
Elizabeth* with Marlene Dietrich, who was bound for Cherbourg.

But Richard was to miss his next concert at the New York
Town Hall, due to his recurring throat trouble.

The Stanhope,
New York
16th December 1946.

Dearest Heart Esther,

Here I am again at home tonight, when I should be at the Town
Hall singing! No sweety, I did not make it after all. I am quite
glad about it because I would not have sung well at all—and it is
better not to sing when I am in this state. I can't afford a "not-so-
big-a-success," after my triumph at Carnegie Hall.

I really feel so miserable and unhappy and I wish the whole
thing were over, and I were home again. Often, really often, I get
so restless and irritable that I want to take the next boat home and
forget all this unhappiness here. I am very bitter, very often! And
it is no pleasure for anyone to be with me at the moment.

When you get this, Christmas will almost be there. Then the
end of the year will come, with hopes and wishes for the new concert . . . 1947 . . . what shall I wish you? Only that my wishes
and yours are the same and that all our dreams come true. My
hopes and wishes for the next years—when we spend many many
Christmases together again.

Esther dear; the undying love of my life—whatever the future
may bring—God Bless you, my heart.

Oh Esther—how I wish with all my heart—everything for you
. . . everything . . .

Ricci!

A return visit to Canada followed, with a concert in Toronto,
and then Richard managed to arrange a concert tour of Central
and South America. It was a tough, hard-hitting whistle-stop tour
of blisteringly hot countries, for which he was ill-prepared.

Advance publicity had given him an enormous build-up, and on
his arrival in Trinidad he found himself billed as "Sir" Richard
Tauber. Caracas, Trinidad and San Juan followed, and he took
thousands of feet of colour film.

He was still depressed, and the tour was wearing him down.
He wrote from Colombia to Diana, who had arrived in England
by now.

Dearest love Diana,

Time goes on and I have one big desire only to be back in New
York in my sitting room. I am so closed up here from the world
with no hope of telephoning. Everything is so old-fashioned and
dirty, noisy and untidy. I hate everything. Why have I to go
through all this? Why, when my success is 100%? I am rather
depressed and unhappy. It is rather like before an operation.

Your loving husband,
Richard.

Caracas, Venezuela,
Sunday 9th February 1947.

Dearest Diana love,

I feel that everything is quite impossible; the journeys, the heat,
the noise, the part-arrangement of the concert makes me feel that I
am in a completely different world.

The halls and the concerts are a great success. Some of the concerts are the longest I have ever done, but otherwise everything
is impossible, unthinkable, out of the world. You have the feeling

that you are out of civilisation. Why do I have to go through this? I am really very miserable and depressed, and longing for the day I go home. My love and thoughts, Diana, dear, with very very deep feeling.

Ever your husband,
Richard.

The next letter was to Esther.

The Condado Beach Hotel,
San Juan,
Puerto Rico.
25th February 1947.

Dearest Heart Esther,

To make you see what life is like here for me, I must tell you that we leave tomorrow morning for Trujillo, and then drive for eighteen miles to the Hotel for one night, then next morning, the 27th, up at 9.00 a.m. for a four-hour flight to Cuba. One night there, and then on to Kingston.

Anyway, the tour is nearing its end and its been like this for six weeks. From Kingston four hours to Miami, and then six hours to New York—and I look forward to reading letters from you which I hope await me there.

Don't forget that I love you.

The temperature is still about 90°—and so much is my love for you.

Your loving,
Ricci.

And from Detroit he wrote Diana:

Detroit,
22nd March 1947.

Dearest Diana heart,

Only a few days now, and I'm on my way home. It is impossible to write to you what I've been through. When I arrive in

England on 12th April I'll tell you. However, I have had one of the greatest successes of my life here, but I also got the biggest shock of my life too. I still owe 14,000 dollars to the backers of *Yours is my Heart*—remember the ones who lent me the money to carry on with the show in New York. I had to pay 4,000 dollars yesterday, and the remaining 10,000 from my money in London. (Ha, ha— what money?)

Nothing has been spared me these last eight months.

I fly back to London to begin rehearsals for *The Birdseller*. Then four to six weeks in the provinces, and we open in London in June. Then in June, I have 24 recordings to do, and I start my BBC Sunday evening broadcasts again.

I love you very much and I am longing to see you. Take care of yourself and don't be so "boom-boom."

Your rather knocked-about husband,
Richard.

Back in New York, before his return to London, he wrote Esther:

The Stanhope,
New York.
1st April 1947.

Dearest Esther heart!

Only a few days, and I will be home and with you again!

Everything seems like a bad dream and almost unreal!

I still have to fight through the last moments here, and things on my return to New York aren't as smooth as I'd hoped they'd be.

Well darling, I will be brave until the end—

God bless you my love. There is nothing more to say before I am back. Nothing that could not wait till I sit beside you again!

So long my dearest heart! Oh, how I long to be back and seeing you again, my love.

Yours,
Ricci.

XVI
SYMPTOMS OF ILLNESS—AND DESPAIR

Diana had returned to Germany on active duty after her leave, to obtain her demob papers.

Richard arrived back in England on April 11th 1947 and was met at the airport by Esther and Irene Ambrus, who was to star with Adèle Dixon in *The Birdseller* at the Palace Theatre. Richard was to conduct, as a follow-up to his successful *Gay Rosalinda*.

"I got the majority of the backers for *The Birdseller*", Irene Ambrus told me, "and Bernard Delfont presented it. Ernst Stern Did the costumes—I knew him from Germany, where he had done some of the most beautiful productions. He did breathtaking designs for *The Birdseller*. Lovely ones.

"When I met Richard at the airport, I was shocked at his appearance. He had lost a great deal of weight, and I said to Esther 'that man is terribly ill.'

"And then we started rehearsals for the production. One day I saw him on the stairs of the orchestra pit. He was coughing—he didn't know how ill he was. I said to his secretary Alexa: 'Look, that man is terribly, terribly ill. You'll have to take him to a doctor for an x-ray. But Richard wouldn't go. When I saw that man killing himself and not knowing it, it broke my heart, and there was nothing I could do."

Esther said that he couldn't make the stairs to his dressing room on the first floor. "His breathing had become very bad, so I arranged to have the artistes' quick-change room on the prompt side of the stage converted to a dressing room for him. From there he could step into the lift to take him down to the orchestra pit."

"When Ivor Novello was playing *King's Rhapsody*, he had the same little room. 'Esther,' he said when I went back to see him, 'you must be very brave coming into this room; the last room Richard had.' A month later Ivor passed away. That was the last dressing room that he had, too."

Even though Richard was contracted to conduct *The Birdseller*, his financial worries were far from over. That didn't stop him from taking a suite at Grosvenor House however. From there he wrote to Diana in Germany:

Grosvenor House,
London, 14th May 1947.

Darling Diana,

Oh let me thank you for all your dear letters which I read with great joy and sentiment. I am rather upset and my feelings are unclear and difficult. When I see you next time I will tell you a nice long story of my heart. You are the only one I really know I can talk to from my soul.

Well, the first night of *The Birdseller* will be over soon and I shall be very occupied. My thoughts will have no time to wander nor to worry. What then? I don't yet know. I wish I did. I so long for you, my darling. I always will. That's me. I am very low and I feel the strain of my unfortunate time in America much more.

The nights have become so frightening that I wake up in the middle of the night sweating with fear. But don't worry, my dearest heart, I will get over it.

Your loving husband,
Richard.

The Birdseller opened with Adèle Dixon, Irene Ambrus, James Etherington and Douglas Byng on May 29th 1947, in the middle of a sweltering heatwave the like of which Londoners hadn't experienced for a long time. The *Daily Telegraph* reported the opening night the following morning: "In his operetta *The Bird-seller*, presented last night at the Palace Theatre, the Viennese composer Karl Zeller has written three lilting waltz tunes which are likely to remain long in the memory. That is more than can be said for the libretto. The theme was said to be Austrian in the 1850s, with the Emperor Franz Josef and his Empress as leading characters. But it was soon clear that the country was none other than familiar Ruritania. With comedy, like originality, notably absent from the plot, it was left to music to save the evening. That was almost achieved by Zeller's rich score and some fine singing, particularly from Adèle Dixon, who acted delightfully. The orchestra was conducted with zest by Richard Tauber; the production was by Dennis Arundell; and the settings by Ernst Stern. There was a delightful ballet arranged by Pauline Grant to traditional Tyrolean music."

But the heatwave caused audiences to dwindle and Richard, who foresaw an early closing for the show, relinquished his £40-a-week suite at Grosvenor House in exchange for a flat in Park West, in London's Edgware Road, for £9 a week. Esther had a flat on the floor below him.

Now confused and frustrated by the repeat of his New York failure, Richard wrote to Diana in Germany practically daily.

Grosvenor House,
20th June 1947.

Dearest love Diana,

I received all your letters, but I can't answer them for I am so mixed up and downhearted, for I cannot find the concentration for all the things that have to be considered and decided. I have never been in such a mess in my life before. Tomorrow morning I am leaving to take a small flat in Park West. I feel it is terrible, but it has to be done. I also found a flat in the building for Alexa, and also for Esther who I have to look after.

I can't express my feelings. Please understand that I am really a dead-loss at the moment.

The show will come off in three weeks time and I shall be on the road again. God Bless you my darling. I still have to be very careful with my diet. Look after yourself.

297 Park West,
3rd July 1947.

Dearest Diana Heart,

Please don't ask me to write you a long letter, I just can't. The temperature is 92° and the sweat simply pours off me. The doctor let me know about my diet, but he thinks there is nothing to worry about. I don't know how the show will run with this weather. We may close in three to four weeks time if business does not pick up.

It was nice to hear your dear voice again.

So long my darling heart.

297 Park West,
4th July 1947.

Dearest Diana,

Well, it's over. *The Birdseller* and another dream has died. I would like to write you my feelings and emotions, but I just can't. I am in a kind of depression where I do not know why I go to bed and why I get up again. I have no fight to see it through, but then I have no fight left in me.

My new flat is very sweet and cosy, very quiet and away from the noise. Alexa looks after me very well, and she and Esther are here when I want them. But honestly I do not want her, or to see anybody. What I am going to do I just don't know. Everything is so mixed up and uncertain. Where is the future? Where and how?

All my loving thoughts.

297 Park West,
5th July 1947.

Dearest Heart,

I just put the receiver down after talking to you, and I feel better. Today is the last performance of *The Birdseller*, and you can imagine how I feel. I have no energy or will-power to do or say anything for the moment, and I know there are many important decisions to make. But I just can't make them. You are so sweet and a real darling. You always understand my position. Thank you for it.

My next concert programme is rather unsettled and uncertain. My BBC radio broadcasts start on Sunday 20th July at 9.30 in the evening. Of course I can't live on this money alone, particularly with these taxes to pay, so I hope to find more work. I am going to Plymouth and then the following week to Morecambe with a recital, but I have to be in London for the BBC recording on the Sunday in between.

Love and dearest thoughts, my love,

297 Park West,
23rd July 1947.

Dearest Diana Heart,

There is not much progress because nothing happens, and my life is so empty and impossible. I sleep badly, for this cough disturbs me, and I have to keep lying down. It's terrible that this show *The Birdseller* had to break down. It upset my whole life. I just can't explain how I feel, but I know that I am not living anymore. Just existing.

The tax people are not very nice either. They want me to pay 50%, 60% and 75% on all my income. 50% from the first £500 I earn in a month, 60% on £800, and so on up to 75%. But the worst thing is that I don't get rid of my chest problem. The three doctors keep telling me that I have bronchitis.

To which Diana replied:

Meppen, Germany.
August 1947.

My sweetie pie,

Your letters should not be so sad. I am sure all will be well. Don't bother about Esther, darling. She is young and as she is there in her flat when you want her it's nice company for you, and Alexa is there to help you all the time.

I will stay here as long as it is convenient for us and you have managed to sort out your separation with Esther. But I do not

think it matters any more. Why should you bother? A friend is a
friend even though she was once a lover. We are living in a different age, sweetie. These things do not matter any more.

I shall be making myself useful as I am organising schools in
England for Polish Prisoner of War children and those from the
Warsaw uprising.

Keep cheerful, my darling, I am sure all these bad things will
pass and a sunny day will shine again for you. After all, schnappie,
you are still young and full of vitality and emotions, so you will
pull yourself together and get over all these troubles quite soon.
You have had worse illnesses. Remember your big illness in '29?
You thought then it was the end of the world, but it wasn't, was
it? I think you might discuss with the doctors the possibilities of a
slight attack of that old illness. Perhaps it is a slight attack of the
chest muscles the way it attacked your hands and knees. It might
be worth asking the doctor from Pistyan to see you (he is in Wales
at the moment).

All my love to you. I think about you dearly, and do not worry
about the money for operations or treatments. I can find £600 for
you at twenty-four hours notice.

All love always,

Your loving wife,
Diana.

Park West,
5th August 1947.

Dearest Diana love,

I could not get through to you in Germany from Plymouth,
darling. I tried for two days, but nothing doing. I arrived this
morning to find your three letters—thank you darling.

I have my BBC programme tonight and am off to Morecambe
for a concert for one week. I do not feel too well and I hope that I
can keep going. It is very important that I earn good money in the
next few weeks. I may need it in case something serious happens
and I have to have something done about my chest. I am under
observation and a decision will be made about what can be done

when I get back. They have to look down into my chest with a stereoscope to see what is going on. Rather nasty. But the x-ray only shows that there is something not in order with the tubes which may be a blister, but they can't say.

I am singing all right, but I suffer all the time. Well, dear heart, sorry I can't write a more cheerful letter, because it's just not in me. I hope there will be better times for us. I wish it with all my heart.

So long love, I think of you dearly and remain your husband,

Richard.

Richard, Alexa and Percy Kahn, his accompanist, were in Plymouth for one of Richard's recitals, "We were walking along the front", recalled Alexa, "and suddenly there was the most strange silence. It was uncanny. And frightening. Richard really wasn't well, and I thought Diana should know, so I wrote to her in Germany."

When Diana got Alexa's letter, she wrote to Richard at once:

Meppen, Germany.
10th August 1947.

My darling sweet,

I am terribly worried about you, and Alexa worried me even more when she wrote that you were suffering terribly during the week in Plymouth. I feel so terrible staying here in Germany, and you are so ill, but I know that it is not my wish, and one word from you and I would take the next plane to England. In any case I am coming to London on the 13th or 14th for two days only as I am going to see your doctor myself. I will not stay here and worry about you from morning to night without seeing you.

So darling, don't worry about Esther, I shall stay those two days in the Dorchester in a small room which I will pay for myself. In any case if you order and eat nothing, the bill is nothing. I shall be there only two days. I arrive about the 13th, and return the 16th, but at least I shall have the feeling that I have seen you.

Your loving wife,
Diana.

Esther was passing through a corridor back-stage during the run of *The Birdseller*, when a swing door burst open and hit her nose. It was Richard on the other side, rushing towards the orchestra pit for the overture. He apologized profusely, and hurried on. But that small accident was to lead to the diagnosis of his fatal illness.

After his television appearance at Alexandra Palace on July 22nd, Esther, who had arranged to have her nose x-rayed on the 25th, persuaded Richard to go along with her to his ear, nose and throat surgeon to have his throat and lungs x-rayed at the same time.

Richard's specialist, recalled that Richard was not a smoker, but he liked the odd cigar, particularly on the days when he didn't have to perform.

"In July 1947," the Doctor told me from his Harley Street surgery, when I asked him what circumstances led to his contacting the surgeon, "symptoms appeared which made it necessary to have Richard's chest examined by x-ray. Unfortunately, it was obvious that he was suffering from a malignant disease, from a cancerous condition of the lung. The only thing to do was to recommend an operation, and I referred him to the surgeon, Lord Brock. It was clear that one lung had to be sacrificed if any attempt was to be made to save him at all."

But Richard believed he had an abcess of the lung.

"Esther, tell me the truth," he said when she returned with the results of the x-rays, "have I got cancer?"

"Whatever made you think that?" she smiled concealingly. "You've only got a little trouble with your chest."

XVII
DARK PASSAGE TO ETERNITY

Richard's coughing attacks had grown worse. Plans were going ahead for a tour of Switzerland and Australia, and Alexa had booked passages for the fulfilment of a new £25,000 contract. It seemed that Richard's financial worries were over at last. But his health anxieties were not.

In the meantime, Richard had learnt that his beloved Vienna State Opera company had announced a guest season at the Royal Opera House, Covent Garden. He found that his old Austrian friend and colleague, Professor Josef Krips, was conducting, and contacted the then Administrator of Covent Garden, Sir David Webster, at once.

"In September 1947," said Sir David, "just a little more than a year after the opera house was re-opened at the end of the war, we invited the Vienna State Opera here. It was the first time in its history that the entire company had taken a repertoire of works outside Vienna.

"Tauber wrote me a letter asking if he could possibly sing in one of his great Viennese successes. I said that the company were my guests, I wasn't in control of them; but I would see what I could do. So I talked to the Viennese and said that I knew it would mean a great deal to Tauber to appear with his former company—and so on the last night of the season he appeared in *Don Giovanni* with Elisabeth Schwarzkopf, Paul Schoeffler, Erich Kunz and Hilde Gueden. He was not absolutely well at the time—as a matter of fact he sang the rôle virtually on one lung, due to the cancer, and I can remember the perspiration flowing from his face. But he gave a very great performance."

When Diana returned to London from Germany and met Richard, whom she had not seen for two months, she was shocked at his appearance. He had lost weight, and the old bounce and gaiety had gone.

A few days before the operation for the removal of the lung, Richard, Diana and Esther went to a cinema and dined together afterwards. The atmosphere was heavy with concealed despair; Diana and Esther sharing their mutual anxiety; Richard strung up in anticipation of the outcome of the meeting between the two women he loved.

Richard and Esther continued to live in Park West, and Diana rented a house in Chelsea. But money was short, even though the contract for the forthcoming tour promised to resolve all their difficulties.

Richard telephoned Irene Ambrus from Park West, and told her he wanted to see her. He admitted to being in terrible financial trouble, and asked her to come over right away.

"As he opened the door," said Irene Ambrus, "I realized that this was a dying man. He asked whether I could raise some money —he didn't have a farthing. I went to many people to see if they would be prepared to help Richard, but none of them did. One even said that he had already given £5,000 to charity that year, and that was his quota.

"When I got home I told my husband that I had seen Tauber dying. He was amazed when I explained that I had only seen half his face, that one side of his face had disappeared. I knew the end was near."

Richard had been under exclusive recording contract to Parlophone and Odeon Records, now owned by EMI, ever since he began recording in the twenties, and asked Diana to borrow some money from Parlophone in advance of royalties.

Diana contacted Parlophone's Dr Oscar Preuss, a life-long friend of Richard's who immediately arranged for the advance. But the entire £1,000 was swallowed up by doctors bills and hospital fees, and left nothing for Richard's specialist and surgeon, who were never to be paid their £400 outstanding fees.

There was, too, the rent for Mara Losseff's flat, which had

fallen into arrears. Richard had remained close to Mara, and took care of her till the end; but now, caught in the web of the triangle he had woven round himself, anxious about his health and his forthcoming performance at Covent Garden, where he was to sing opera for the first time in seven years, he was in a turmoil.

He owed £22,000 to the Inland Revenue. After his death all income on his royalties was frozen until this debt was paid. Diana was to be left penniless, and had to wait fourteen years, until the income-tax debt was finally paid, before she received a penny from royalties.

Esther, Mara and Alexa were also left without support, and it took them years to find their feet. How their lives were to change after the death of their beloved Richard . . .

"Once when Richard was struggling for breath, and had upset me, I felt it better to stay away," Diana said. "I walked for hours in the park. When I returned home to my mother, miserable and with tears in my eyes, for I knew he was dying, my mother said: 'Richard hasn't been off the telephone, Diana. He is so worried about you. He wanted to know why you left him alone for so long.'

"I telephoned him at once. 'Oh Sweetie, sweetie, where are you?' he cried in desperation. 'I'm so mixed up. So mixed up and torn between myself and everything around me.'

"Poor Richard; this turmoil—Esther and Mara and me—was too much for such an ill man. Esther and I both tried to understand each other and became friends in our common misery and anxiety."

"But he couldn't stand Mara's drinking any more," Esther added. "He had sent her to wonderful homes to cure her drinking, but she used to bribe the nurses to bring her drink."

Yet what had there been in his association with Mara? Even though he was married to Diana, and living with Esther, he would still visit Mara regularly. What was there in this relationship—this bond—that had held firm until now? Perhaps the answer is that she was part of Richard's *glorious years* when he was young and rich and had the German public at his feet, and there was nothing Diana or Esther could do to diminish this tie.

Mara represented the beloved countries Richard had lost—
Germany and, subsequently, Austria. She was his last link with his
past, and he hung on to it. She spoke fluent German and played the
piano beautifully. When he visited her, she sang his old German
songs. She was the perfect companion who made no demands.

The fact that they had never consummated their love contributed to Richard's deep-rooted sense of responsibility towards
Mara, and it took their friends a long time to understand his close
attachment to this beautiful woman.

Mara had been a cosy person, a good cook, and a home-lover.
When Diana asked Richard why he hadn't married her, he said
that he couldn't stand her drinking, and in the end it destroyed his
love for her.

"Then I realized, as Mara herself had told me many years
before," Diana said, "that Mara had drunk moderately when she
first fell in love with Richard, but when he married me, and later
met Esther, her drinking got worse. She naturally felt that she was
losing him for good; but she needn't have worried, for Richard
was never to forsake her.

"At Richard's Requiem Mass, Mara looked utterly unhappy.
She was stone-cold-sober, devoid of make-up, and she was still
outstandingly beautiful."

"So," Diana continued, returning to the days before the
operation, "the situation was fraught with hidden emotions, and
yet all the time Esther and I had to keep a brave face for the
ultimate end, as we both knew it was near. And we would both
lose him."

On September 15th Richard spent the night at Nuffield House
under observation, and the doctors came to the conclusion that he
had advanced cancer of the lung.

"Richard was told that there would have to be an operation,"
said Diana, "but he didn't ask for details, although I had been told
that one lung would have to be removed. In a way, he was afraid
to know.

"I stayed with my mother that evening, and cried myself to
sleep.

"But before the operation Richard said, 'I am going to sing. I have promised Professor Krips. I must and I will sing this performance, and nothing in the world will stop me. Afterwards they can do what they like with me.' "

And on Saturday September 27th 1947, he sang Don Ottavio in *Don Giovanni* at Covent Garden, to a tumultuous reception. Apart from those close to him, no one knew that they were witnessing the tragic farewell of one of the finest Mozart singers of his time.

The following day he was to sing again. He had two more half-hour radio programmes to complete for the BBC before he entered hospital.

"Earlier on," said BBC producer Ronnie Waldman, "we had begun to grow more and more concerned about the obvious trouble Richard had been having with his throat. There had been two occasions—one in 1945, when we'd had to cancel the programme, and now towards the end of 1947, when it became known that he would have to go into hospital.

"We came to the planning stages of the last programme in the series. It was decided that it would be safer to do the penultimate programme of the series 'live,' and then record the final programme on the same day, and broadcast it the following Sunday.

"It was asking a lot of him, I know, to do two programmes on one day, particularly since he would have sung at Covent Garden the night before, but we had discussed it with his friends and doctors, and they felt that since he was going into hospital during the week, between the two final programmes, it was the only way we could do it.

"The emotion in the studio on the recording of the last programme was electrifying. You could have cut it with a knife. Yet I don't think any of us knew that we would never be working with Richard again."

Alexa Weir, Richard's secretary and confidante was one of his most faithful colleagues. She had travelled with him to South Africa and to North, South and Central America, where in the sweltering heat she would stand on the side of the stage with fresh shirts for him to change into between items. She too had a flat in Park West, in which he had an office, and since she was both tactful and sincere, Richard could give her his total confidence.

Alexa vividly remembers Richard's last recording for the BBC. "We'd been along to rehearsals with the Melachrino Orchestra on the Sunday," Alexa said, "the day after his Covent Garden appearance. He had his usual little rest in the dressing room. And a little fit of coughing of course. He ate very little, and the rehearsal continued right until the run-through. And then the show was ready to go on the air.

"It was a very sad time, the last few weeks. I was all right until the time the 'On the Air' red light came on, and then I just couldn't stay in the dressing room. I had to go out. It was just too much. And I went outside to hear what was going on. I can remember walking up and down the corridor looking at my watch, just counting the minutes. And then the closing signature tune 'You Are My Heart's Delight' came up, and I said 'Thank God—that was the last one.' A feeling of gratitude came over me—gratitude to God that he'd got through it. That he'd really finished it."

Alexa collected his music from the studio, and went back to the dressing room with him to collect his belongings. "I would always hear him say 'Good bye' to his things, but on this occasion he made a very prophetic remark: 'Ah well,' he said, 'now my work is over.' He put his hands on to his piano, and said, 'Well, goodbye piano,' and with that he put on his hat and went from the BBC."

He entered Guy's Hospital the following Wednesday, and the operation for the removal of the lung was performed the following day.

"As he lay there, his blue eyes looked so sweetly at me, slightly blurred from the first sedative injection," Diana said. "Are you sure you're all right?' I asked rather stupidly, and he smiled back at me.

" 'Mi Mi Mi Mi,' I heard him trying out his voice along the corridor as he was wheeled to the operating theatre.

"I couldn't stay in the hospital, so I drove round London in a taxi. I went to Professor Josef Krips' hotel and told him about the operation. He was shattered. He had had no idea when Richard sang the week before that he was so ill. That one lung had disintegrated. I could see the tears well into his eyes.

"I returned to the hospital, and five and a half hours later, Richard was brought back to his ward. 'Have you saved him?' I asked the surgeon. 'We've removed one lung, but we have to send a tissue away to be tested.' he replied. I knew by his face that Richard was doomed. They had been unable to save the other lung, the cancer had gone too far.

"Suddenly the nurse looking after Richard hurried up to me. 'Mrs Tauber, please come. He is asking for you.' I remember saying: 'Nurse, are you sure it is—me—he is calling for?' And not Esther. 'He's calling Diana, Diana, Diana,' the nurse replied.

" 'Thank you for coming,' Richard said gripping my hand. 'Where are the other poor schnappulas?'—meaning Esther and Alexa. I told him they were waiting at Park West. His eyes were so blue and kind, I had the greatest difficulty in not weeping before him. I held his hand until my hands became numb. He fell asleep, and I stayed with him till morning."

The following day Richard again asked for Esther. Letters and telegrams arrived from well-wishers from all over the world. One of the first was from Sir Charles B. Cochran, who had presented Richard in *Paganini*.

Charles B. Cochran,
49 Old Bond Street,
London W.

My dear Richard,

I was distressed to hear that you were laid low, and pray that you are making a good and speedy recovery.

Few things have given me greater happiness than to hear your splendid performance in *Don Giovanni*. *Unquestionably* you must return to Opera when you get well—you showed up a lot of people. After all, there are very few people able to sing Mozart.

Affectionate regards from Evelyn and myself,

Yours as ever,
Charles B. Cochran.

After leaving hospital, Richard went for his second check-up one afternoon, and he and Esther dined with Irene Ambrus that evening. "I had a few people over," said Irene Ambrus, "and naturally there was wine and cigars, and Richard said he was allowed to have anything—a cigar, wine—any kind of food he liked.

"And then there was a heart-breaking moment when he brought out the programme for his Australian tour, which had been planned for later that year. He discussed what he was going to sing with great excitement, and while he was talking to the others, Esther drew me aside into the bedroom and said she wanted to tell me something.

"The doctor had told her that afternoon that Richard had only three to four weeks to live. A cold shiver ran down my spine. Richard was talking about the great news of his Australian programme in the drawing room—and we were discussing his dying in my bedroom."

Vigil

On November 20th 1947 Richard was sufficiently recovered to go with Esther to Torquay, where he convalesced at the Imperial Hotel. His financial position was worse than ever, even though he stayed in a £70-a-week suite. He returned to London on December 13th, but the coughing fits started again, and he was admitted to Guy's Hospital; but he grew restless and discharged himself after ten days.

"Goodness me," Esther exclaimed when he walked into her flat at Park West, "What are you doing here?" "I can't stand being in hospital, darling, I must be with you. I must be with you," he replied.

A further examination eventually revealed that the other lung was affected, and that there was no hope of recovery.

However, he practised with Percy Kahn every day. The coughing attacks became more serious and difficult to overcome. Doctors drew the fluid which had formed in the lung cavity, and so eased his breathing for a few days at a time, but then it would start all over again.

On Wednesday January 7th Richard, Diana, Esther and Alexa were at Park West, Esther was cooking—grilled steak, boiled rice and vegetables.

Then Richard, barely able to breathe, whispered: 'I feel ill. I must see the doctor.' Diana telephoned Doctor Wornum, who said he would arrange for a bed at the London Clinic at once.

"I remember adding: 'Please don't forget the telephone and a radio,'" Diana said, "Though in my heart I knew that Richard would never use his beloved telephone again, nor hear the radio."

Richard was helped into his wheelchair, and wheeled along the corridor to the lift and the waiting car downstairs. Diana sat in the front and Richard and Esther behind. Alexa stood on the steps of Park West, waving Richard off.

After the short, silent journey to the London Clinic, Richard was wheeled into the lift. Before the lift stopped, he braced himself with the courage he had shown through his first operation.

Diana and Esther helped Richard into a chair in his private ward. He was breathing with extreme difficulty, and Esther helped him out of his rehearsal siren-suit.

The Sister arrived, and gave Richard oxygen.

"Do you feel better?" Diana asked him. He took the mouthpiece away from his face and smiled: 'You'll laugh at this; but I do!'"

Richard was put to bed, and given an injection to put him to sleep. "I suggest you both go home now, and I will call you if necessary, but he should sleep till morning," the Sister said.

Diana and Esther returned to Park West and had a drink in the bar. In all the weeks before and during Richard's illness and operation, there had never been a word of discord between them, nor any recrimination on either side. Richard seemed to have the capacity for keeping both women in love with him, without arousing their hatred or scorn for one another.

The two women who had shared his most intimate secrets and affection awaited the news. They had each given of themselves, in different ways. Each, a different kind of love and devotion. They each knew that the man who had returned their adoration would soon leave them, never to return. But they were each to hold that part of him dear to them through the coming years, for their lives had been touched with a greatness they were never to experience again.

Diana rang the hospital from the bar of Park West, and was assured that Richard was sleeping peacefully. She went back to Chelsea, emotionally exhausted.

Esther went to bed upstairs.

Diana's telephone rang at 12.30 p.m. It was the London Clinic: "Come at once." Diana was already dressed, expecting the call.

"As soon as I got there, I saw that Richard was dying. I telephoned Esther, but could get no reply. I rang the night porter and urged him to go upstairs and wake her. I sent the car for her."

At one in the morning, Esther was woken by the banging on her door. The telephone had rung several times, but she had been in a deep sleep. She opened the door to the porter, who told her Diana had sent the car for her. She was to go to the Clinic at once.

Diana sat with Richard, watching the last minutes of his life slip by.

Esther arrived. She wiped the perspiration from Richard's face and hands, but he never regained consciousness.

Diana sent for the priest from the nearby church in Spanish Place. As he entered the room, Esther left.

The two women who had shared Richard's happiest hours had shared his dying moments.

"I sat on one side of the bed with the nurse and held Richard's pale, limp hand," Diana said, "till the nurse said 'He's gone.'"

A Requiem Mass took place at St James, Spanish Place, London, on January 12th 1948, and Richard was buried at the Brompton Cemetery.

On January 20th, at the end of a Memorial Concert at the Albert Hall, with the London Philharmonic Orchestra and the BBC Theatre Orchestra conducted by Sir Adrian Boult and Walter Goehr, seven thousand friends rose to sing 'You Are My Heart's Delight' with the Luton Girls Choir, as a final tribute to a man whose voice had thrilled millions—and continues to do so.

INDEX

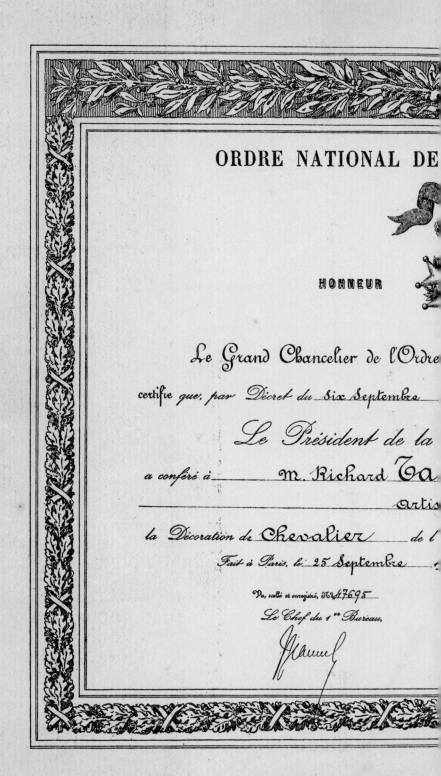

ORDRE NATIONAL DE

HONNEUR

Le Grand Chancelier de l'Ordre

certifie que, par Décret du Six Septembre

Le Président de la

a conféré à ——— M. Richard Va

artis

la Décoration de Chevalier de l

Fait à Paris, le 25 Septembre

Vu, scellé et enregistré, N° A 7695

Le Chef du 1er Bureau,